How To Quit Your Job — The Right Way

A 5-Step Plan To Ditching Your Day Job

Danny Iny

Jim Hopkinson

Questions

Questions can be sent to support@mirasee.com.

Dedicated to those with the courage and conviction to make the leap.

Quit Your Job Extras

Free PDF Downloads +
Online Video Companion Course

When it comes to making the leap, we want to give you all the tools necessary to quit your job the right way. Get free bonus resources and a discounted price to our online video companion course.

Free PDF Downloads
- Danny Iny's bestselling book, *Engagement From Scratch!*
- Full color Ikigai and Zen Diagram charts
- All 10 case studies in PDF form
- Financial inventory template

Online Video Companion Course – 50% off coupon
Are you a visual learner? You'll love our video-based companion course.

- 60+ minutes of video instructions
- Entertaining and educational storytelling
- Video walk-throughs of the 5-step plan

Get your free PDF downloads and course coupon:

http://mrse.co/quit-your-job-extras

Website Links and Further Reading Available Online

To make your reading experience smoother, all links to websites, resources, and articles mentioned in the book are organized by chapter, in order of appearance, on this page:

http://mrse.co/quit-your-job-links

Happy reading!

Contents

Introduction

On a hot summer day in August 2010, a JetBlue flight attendant quit his job. Now, this by itself isn't noteworthy, as there are roughly 100,000 flight attendants in the US, so on any given day, there's a good chance one of them might give notice. But this was different. Spectacularly different.

On that fateful day, the flight attendant later claimed, as the flight on which he was working taxied to a stop, a passenger stood up too early to retrieve their bag from the overhead compartment. Despite repeated warnings to remain seated, the unruly passenger continued to remove the oversized luggage, and in doing so, hit the flight attendant in the head with it. When asked for an apology, the passenger responded with profanity.

Here's what happened next:

1. The flight attendant got on the plane's public address system, swore back at the passenger, and declared, "I Quit!"

2. He grabbed two beers from the plane's beverage cart.

3. He deployed the emergency evacuation slide and dramatically exited the plane in style.

Of course, there are two sides to every story. Specifically, the New York Port Authority Police determined that his entire story was a lie, as none of the dozens of passengers that were interviewed after the incident collaborated with his version of the altercation.

While the story went viral and made for great fodder on social media and late night TV, he was arrested, fined $10,000, officially fired, and I'm assuming, will never work in the industry again.

There's no doubt that this example is a fantastically *memorable* way to quit a job, but if you're looking for a long and fulfilling career, it's definitely not the *right* way to do it.

In this book, *How To Quit Your Job — The Right Way: A 5-Step Plan To Ditching Your Day Job*, we'll show you how to get out of a job you hate, and how to transition into a life with more freedom, flexibility, and money, while doing the work you were meant to do.

This book has two important parts to it.

First, is the 5-step plan:

1. The Wakeup Call — the key moment when you know you've had enough

2. Craft Your Exit Plan — your timeline to make it happen

3. The (Fun) Research — determining what to do next

4. Hustle and Flow — testing your new gig and adjusting when needed

5. Quitting Day — how to exit your day job the right way

The second part is just as important — real life case studies of people that escaped the cubicle and exactly how they did it, showing that this is possible. *It's ok to love what you do.*

You'll hear about Naomi, who restructured her job to fuel her passion for music. You'll see how Alan treated the process like a poker game while he secretly launched his own business. Nathan will confess that he spent four years preparing to leave and explain why he regrets it. These are just a few of the stories we've collected to inspire you and help you plan a smart, elegant transition.

You'll also hear several stories from co-author Jim Hopkinson, the Director of Courses at Mirasee. He will be your primary guide through this process, and he knows where you're coming from. "I've had great jobs and not so great jobs. I've quit jobs, and I've been laid off from jobs. One time, I decided I was going to quit my job, but before I could quit, I got laid off. I've advised a lot of people on their career, and I've seen a lot."

Co-author Danny Iny is the CEO and founder of Mirasee, a company that helps individuals launch businesses they love. "Our team works with entrepreneurs like you who have a product, a service, or a message to share, and a genuine desire to build a business and help others with their unique voice. Or perhaps I should say, *future* entrepreneurs like you, because if you're reading this book, you probably have a day job that you want to get out of so you can do something new, have more freedom, and make more money."

One thing to note: this isn't a book that is going to teach you the intricacies of how to launch and grow your future business. However, you can find a host of free resources at Mirasee.com. Additionally, check out the other books in this *Business Reimagined* series, *Website Copywriting* and *Blog Post Ideas*.

The goal with this book is to get you out of the rut you're in, help you focus on what you want to do, lead you right up to quitting day, and then push you out of the nest. From there, you'll be ready to fly.

Let's get started.

Step 1:
The Wakeup Call

Chapter 1: What's On Your Tombstone?

6:59am

You're blissfully floating through space and time. Well, it's a little bit weird, since you're sitting in the grassy area outside your old college dorm, but instead of your college friends, you're with two co-workers, your mom, and Maggie, the barista from your local coffee shop. It's a sunny day, although for some reason you're wearing your favorite puffy winter jacket, and...

Bzzzz. Bzzzz. Bzzzz.

Now things are fuzzier. Is that a bee buzzing around your head? Why won't it stop? Why won't it go away?

Bzzzz. Bzzzz. Bzzzz.

7:00am

You groggily awake from your dream, and realize the annoying buzzing sound is your vibrating phone on the nightstand next to your head. The puffy jacket is actually your down comforter. You start to wonder why your mom would be hanging out with your work friends and decide it's too early for psychoanalysis.

It's Monday morning. Time to start another workweek.

How does that make you feel?

Are you excited?

Are you ready to jump out of bed like an eager bunny rabbit and tackle the day? Can't wait to get to the office and pick right back up where you left off on Friday?

What? No?

Hmmm, I guess because you're reading this, and the name of the book is *How to Quit Your Job*, that's not the case.

You squint at your phone and poke your finger at the snooze button.

Comedian George Carlin once said, "Oh you hate your job? Why didn't you say so? There's a support group for that. It's called EVERYBODY, and they meet at the bar." (The quote has also been attributed to Drew Carey).

Sadly, to some degree he's right. *Most* people don't like their jobs.

According to Gallup, about 68% of people are not engaged at work. Assuming a five day workweek, that means that about 70% of people are unhappy 70% of their life!

Then they break down that number even further. Of that group, 51% simply say they are "not engaged" at work. Just not into it. To me, that says their job is just "alright." It's "so-so." Once in awhile it's ok, but usually they'd say, "No, I'm not happy."

However, 17% say they're "actively disengaged." To me, that message is pretty clear, "I HATE MY JOB!"

Maybe you're saying, "Well, my job isn't *that* bad. Sure my boss doesn't really respect me, and Tim in finance is a real jerk, but you know, that's why they call it *work*, right?" (You can't even force a smile at your half-hearted joke).

But here's the problem…

Bzzzz. Bzzzz. Bzzzz.

7:09am

Snooze.

You're going to have to will yourself out of bed *again*, and as you get into your beat-up car *again*, and fight stop-and-go traffic *again*, you realize that you haven't had a raise in two years or a real vacation in three.

And so you start thinking about what it could be like…

What if you *loved* your job?
What if you made *great* money?
What if you could work from *anywhere*?

Bzzzz. Bzzzz. Bzzzz.

Stop it. Don't hit snooze. Pay attention. Listen to me.

I repeat: that alarm is going to go off again tomorrow. And the next day. And the day after that.

If you're 28 years old, do you want to hate getting up for another *40 years*?

And I don't care if you're 38 or even 48 years old. It's never too late to change course. In fact, if you're older, you might be in a *better* position to do so because you've got more experience.

When we look at the case studies later in this book, you'll see that most people had a wake-up call moment. A particular event happened in their day job that triggered a response that said, "That's it, I need to leave this job before I go insane. It's just not worth it."

For Andy, it was when his boss hid information from him, leaving him hanging out to dry in the middle of a client meeting. For Naomi, it was the hiring of additional layers of management and a restructuring that would affect her future. For a lot of people, it's just trying to get out of bed on another ordinary Monday, dreading the day, and saying, "Enough."

Let me share a story by James Victore, an award-winning art director, designer, speaker, and author, as told in an article on 99U.com.

> A few years back after one of my more impassioned lectures, a young buck in the back row raised his hand. "Mr. Victore," he said, "I understand what you're saying about taking risks in your career, but I've got rent to pay."

> I was shocked by his defeatist attitude, saddened at how the practicalities of life had already beaten this young creative soul down so that his biggest ambition in life was to pay rent.

> Gone was adventurous youth. This kid was no longer the hero of his own life, willing to face his fears and slay the dragons that kept him from his reward. He was already sheepishly waving a white flag out the window of his minivan.

> "What's your name?" I asked. "Thomas," he said.

"Thomas, here's your tombstone: 'Here lies Thomas, he would have done great work, but he had to pay the rent.'"

So what's it going to be? What's it going to say on *your* tombstone? Are you going to look back on your life and be proud of what you accomplished, or suffer through an exhaustive lifetime of dreadful Monday mornings when you're laying in bed and then…

Bzzzz. Bzzzz. Bzzzz.

Don't look at this as waking up. Look at it as a wake-up call.

Are you ready to quit your job? Let's find out.

Chapter 2: I Hate My Job Because…

There's no doubt, quitting your job can be a really big deal, especially if you have other people counting on you.

So I want to ask you ten questions to make sure you really should be quitting, instead of just fixing something that's currently broken at your present job.

Now if you've already made up your mind, if you're sitting there saying, "Jim, I hate my job so much, I'm ready to light myself on fire," then, by all means, jump ahead to Step 2, Craft Your Exit Plan.

But I recommend you stick with me for a second. Here's why.

We're going to take a minute, look at these ten questions, get clear about your goals, and try to hone in on why you hate your job so much.

These questions are by no means scientific, and you shouldn't base your career plan on a simple quiz, but your answers should steer you into one of the following directions:

1) You pursue some of these alternatives at your current job, things dramatically improve, and you decide to stay there.

If that's the case, no judgment. In fact, we're happy for you. Full-time jobs are not the enemy. Full-time jobs *that you hate* are the enemy.

2) You're *pretty sure* you still want to leave your day job, but you want to make things as comfortable as possible while you're planning that exit.

For example, even if you've got one foot out the door and plan to leave within a year, you might as well get a raise now so that you'll have more money to put toward your emergency fund before you go.

3) It becomes clear that you're *definitely* going to leave your job, and you use the answers to these questions to map out your next step.

Questions to ask before you quit your job

1. Is the work that you do respected and valued by those at work?

2. Are you learning new things and picking up new skills?

3. Are you paid what you are worth based on the work that you do?

4. Did you take this job for the right reasons (not for the money, or because it was a 'hot' industry, or your father-in-law hired you)?

5. Are you using your natural talents on the job?

6. Do you have enough free time to recharge, including weekends and vacation, or are you working an unsustainable amount of hours?

7. If not in your dream job, are you at least on a path that will bring you one step closer to your dream job?

8. Do you have a manager or a mentor that is actively helping further your career?

9. Do you have a manageable commute that doesn't drain your time and energy?

10. Do you pass the pillow test? When you lay your head down on your pillow at night, are you generally satisfied and not stressed about work? When you take your head off the pillow in the morning, are you generally happy to go to work?

Now let's look at a few of the questions and see if there are changes you can make to your current situation.

"I hate my job because my commute is terrible."

Are you losing countless hours every week sitting in grueling traffic? The average commute time in the US is about 25 minutes, but for those in major cities, it's often double that number, or even more. Add in a traffic accident or 8" of snow and you're not making it home on time for dinner too often.

There's no doubt that losing hours of your day sitting in traffic can dramatically affect the way you look at your job. But the options are pretty clear:

- Ask for a flexible schedule so that you can commute during off-hours or work from home one or more days per week

- Get a new day job that is closer to home

- Pursue a new career that allows you the flexibility to work from anywhere, on your own schedule

"I hate my job because I work too many hours."
If you find yourself working 9, 10, or 12 hours a day, and your friends and family need you to wear a name tag so they remember who you are on the rare occasion they actually see you, it's only a matter of time until you burn out.

Solutions include:

- Delegating more work or hiring an assistant

- Focusing on only the most important tasks that bring you the most joy and the most revenue

- Setting boundaries and carving out free time and vacations to recharge

"I hate my job because I'm broke or underpaid."
Many people generally like their job, their boss, and

their co-workers, but know that they are woefully underpaid.

Studies show that more than half of all workers did not negotiate their last salary, and people are generally afraid to ask for a raise because they've never been taught how to do it.

The solutions are straightforward:

- Ask for a raise at your current job
- Find a better paying day job
- Create a business where you control how much you make

Resource: Co-author Jim offers free salary negotiation tips at SalaryTutor.com.

"I hate my job because I'm bored, underutilized, and/or not doing something I love."
Do you love the outdoors but find yourself stuck in a cubicle? Do you have a Masters degree but are assigned entry-level work?

One solution might be to mix things up:

- Offer to take on more responsibility

- Ask to transfer to a new department

- Volunteer for that new initiative and learn a new skill

You don't get what you don't ask for
The first takeaway here is a simple word. ASK.

I've had several conversations that went like this:

"I really wish I could work from home two days a week."
Jim: "Have you *asked* about working remotely?"

"I really wish my boss had picked me for that new project."
Jim: "Did you *tell her* you were interested?"

"I really wish my manager would give me a raise."
Jim: "Have you *asked* your manager for a raise?"

You get the idea. Your boss can't read your mind.

So if you're thinking about staying at your current job, here's what you're going to do.

Tell your boss exactly what you want.

After all, at this point, there's no downside — you're probably quitting anyway! You have nothing to lose, and you might be surprised at the answer.

Focus on what is important to you
Look back at the ten questions you just answered.

Which ones resonated with you the most?
What was most important to you?

Whether you decide to pursue another day job or go out on your own, the last thing you want to do is take the things you hate about your current job and carry them over to your next gig after you quit.

So look at the list again and think about the elements that you might want in your next job:

- The ability to work from anywhere, on a schedule you decide, without a commute

- Working fewer hours and spending more time doing the things you want

- Earning a comfortable salary and being paid what you're worth

- Doing something that you were meant to do, that you love to do, and that benefits others

Which way are you running?

One question you can ask yourself is, "Are you running *away* from something, or are you running *toward* something?"

For example, let's say you're an accountant. You have an analytical brain, love the process of making numbers work, and have an unhealthy obsession with spreadsheets.

Sometimes it's ok to run away from something — a terrible boss, a low salary, a dead-end path to advancement — and take another accounting job. You're content and confident in what you do; there's just a specific situation in your current workplace that needs to change.

But an alternative situation is to be running toward something. Let's say your job as an accountant is OK, but the truth is that you really hate the rules and restrictions of the job. You don't like being stuck in an office, feel like you're not making a difference, and you only majored in accounting because your parents wanted you to "study something safe that would pay well and always be in demand."

Deep down, you feel your calling is to be a life coach. It would mean explaining this to your family, going back for more training and education, and potentially earning a lot less money while building your business. But at the end of your career when you look back at your life, is that a goal worth running toward?

You've come to the end of Step 1. Have you had a wake-up call moment yet?

We've given you some things to think about, so take some time to decide whether you should adjust something in your current job, or prepare to abandon ship.

If you're ready to move on, let's craft your exit plan.

Step 2:
Craft Your Exit Plan

Chapter 3: The Importance of Planning

Let me pose a question. What do you think is more important? Figuring out what to do or figuring out how and when to do it?

It's a classic left brain vs. right brain dilemma, and if I'm honest for a second, in writing this book, I struggled for a bit deciding which to put first.

To the creative dreamers out there that can't wait to figure out their next step, you might be saying, "How can I set a timeline on a plan if I have no idea what I want to do?"

And if you're firmly in that camp, then yes, you have my permission to go ahead and jump to Step 3. Find out what you want to do with your life, and then come back here afterward to see how to put that plan into place.

But once again, my recommendation is to stick with me and map out a plan of action first. Here's why:

1. A goal without a plan is just a wish

Let's take that a step further. Author and motivational speaker Greg S. Reid has said:

> A dream written down with a date becomes a goal.
> A goal broken down into steps becomes a plan.
> A plan backed by action makes your dreams come true.

Trust me, there are lots of people that *dream* of leaving their job. They talk a good game, even painting a very detailed picture to their co-workers during lunch. "Just you wait and see! One day I'm going to leave all you losers here at our law firm that writes the fine print on the warning labels that go on somewhat dangerous garden tools, and I'm going to write an Oscar-winning screenplay for my movie *Earthworm*."

But instead of working on that sure-to-be-a-hit screenplay during that lunch break, they just like to talk about it. Committing to a goal with a date makes it real.

2. Having a framework gives you confidence

Putting a plan into place frees your mind to focus on what's important in the coming months: finding out what you want to do and determining your next steps.

If you're just winging it, you're constantly going to be asking yourself questions like, "Is now the right time to leave?" and "Am I going to be able to pay my rent?"

Doing the work up front lets you set those fears aside and avoid making irrational decisions. You can plot out exactly what you need to do, and when things get crazy, you can refer back to the plan you put in place.

While I don't want to encourage the thinking that you have to wait until everything in your life is perfect before moving forward — hint, that never happens — going through a checklist and doing a 360-degree inventory of your life will ensure you're ready to take the plunge, and know where any weaknesses might be.

In the next two chapters, we'll do that by looking at your financial well-being, and your emotional well-being.

Chapter 4: Check Your Finances

Before you can plan for the future, it's wise to take stock of your current situation.

The first thing you'll want to address is your financial standing. Like it or not, money is a major consideration, and the reason many people fail is that they run out of cash and need to go back to a steady job.

Sometimes a person in their 50s, with decades of experience — and savings — will shift into a second career. That cash cushion can go a long way toward building a successful business. However, that phase of life might also come with added responsibilities, like a hefty mortgage or kids in college.

Those in their 20s or 30s have their own sets of challenges. While they might have the drive and passion of youth, more freedom to relocate, and fewer overall obligations, they might not have as much experience or earning power, and could be dealing with student loan debt.

Here are three steps to analyze your financial situation:

1. Inventory your expenses

Carve out several hours on a weekend and go through your last six months of expenses, or better yet, the last year. That means looking at your bank statements, thinking about how much cash you take out each week, and analyzing those credit card summaries.

First, look at your fixed expenses. These are things you need to pay each month, no matter what.

They might include:

- Rent or mortgage, plus insurance
- Car payment, gas, parking, and insurance
- Utility bills such as gas and electric
- Health insurance and ongoing medical costs

- Student loans and other payments
- Childcare
- Internet and phone access
- Groceries

Then, add on all your optional or variable expenses each month.

They might include:

- Money for going out, eating at restaurants, and other entertainment
- Trips and vacations
- Clothing
- Subscriptions like Netflix, Dropbox, website tools, cable TV, and gym memberships

Once you're done, tally up all your monthly expenses. If necessary, average things out. For example, if you're looking at a full year, and you bought plane tickets in April, June, and October for a total of $1200, put $100 per month. If your heating bill is $30 during the summer but $130 during the winter, calculate a number that makes sense.

2. Inventory your income and savings

Look at your last few paychecks and calculate your monthly take-home pay (after taxes). Then think about any additional income that you might have when you leave your job, such as vacation pay, commissions due to you, and so on. Finally, look at how much savings you have put away toward this goal.

3. Do the math and adjust as necessary

Let's say you come up with the following:

- Monthly take-home pay of $4,500
- Monthly expenses of $3,500
- A "Quit My Job" fund where you've stashed away about $9,000

Of course, your numbers may differ significantly based on your lifestyle and where you live, but let's use these amounts for now.

Look at your take home pay of $4,500 per month. How does that feel to you? For some people, that's plenty to live on. For others, maybe you'd like to be closer to $6,000, $10,000, or more. Choose a target number for your future business.

Now look at your expenses of $3,500 per month. How does that feel to you? For some, that's totally manageable. For others, sitting down for the first time and truly analyzing your spending is shocking.

Now is a great time, even if it's just in the short term during the transition, to go through that list and eliminate things you don't need or can do without.

Is it time to cut cable TV, eat out less, or cancel the music service you never listen to? Or maybe it's time for more drastic measures, such as moving to a different location with much lower rent or selling your car. If you realize that credit card debt is a major issue right now, some might be best served to put plans on hold until that debt is wiped out.

For this example, let's say you decide $3,500 is a bit high, and you're able to make some sacrifices and cut $500 per month from your bills.

That leaves you with $4,500 in income and $3,000 in expenses, meaning you have $1,500 to sock away in your "Quit My Job" Fund. If you save for six months, you'll have $9,000. Added to the $9,000 you've already saved, you'll have a total of $18,000.

With that amount, you have six months of living expenses once you quit your job. Some people will be fine with less, but ideally, you'll have more.

However, as you'll see later in the *Hustle and Flow* section, the plan is to have consistent income coming in *before* you quit your job, not giving your notice and starting from scratch by tapping into your savings in order to live.

Don't cut too deep

One thing I will add in your quest to streamline your life is to be careful about the things you cut from the budget.

- If you're paying $50 a month for a gym membership and you don't use it, by all means cancel it immediately. But if you go consistently and working out is a way for you to stay healthy, have energy, and eliminate stress, that's a net positive when taking on a new venture.

- If your credit card statement is filled with auto-renewing subscriptions every month, get out the ax and slash expenses where you can. But if there's a must-see Netflix show that you watch with your partner for date night each week, it's probably OK to pay the $9/month for the health of your relationship.

- While it probably makes sense to put that expensive international vacation to Tuscany on hold for now, make sure to leave some room for fun in your budget. Pursuing a new career doesn't mean saying goodbye to your kids, locking yourself in your basement, and working seven days a week. Quite the opposite. Make it a family affair and plan low-cost, rewarding activities as breaks from your hard work.

- Lastly, make sure not to skimp on the things you'll need for your next venture. For example, when I went out on my own in late 2011, the first thing I did was head to the Apple store and upgrade my 3-year-old phone and heavy, slow, aging laptop. It might seem silly to drop $1,700 of my severance pay the week after leaving the safety and income of a full-time job, but I knew that investing in technology would help me work faster and more efficiently in my new business. In fact, I wrote this book with the same Macbook Air I purchased five years ago.

Financial Craziness

As we conclude this chapter, I want to emphasize that money is a *crazy* subject for many people, so your level of comfort will vary dramatically. For some careers and locations, earning $4,000 per month is enough to live comfortably doing what you love to do. In a place like San Francisco, that amount will barely cover a decent apartment to live in, before even considering any other expenses. For some people, money is a crucial measuring stick for success. For others, the quest for more and more cash just isn't that important.

We're not financial planners, so consult someone you trust. The numbers used in the example are simply to show you a rough framework and get you thinking about doing the inventory and getting a handle on where you stand before you move forward.

So work backward to determine what you need, how much cash you have in the bank, and determine what works for you.

Chapter 5: The Mind-Body Connection

While it's important to do a 360° inventory on your financial well-being, don't neglect your emotional or physical well-being, or the essential people in your life.

Baseball player Yogi Berra once said, "Ninety percent of this game is half mental." While that might be a tough message to decipher, what's true is that your mindset and emotions play a critical role in your success. Let's look at three elements that you should "get your head around" before you start.

1) Mental well-being

Step back and really reflect if this is the right time mentally for you to make this move. It's not going to be easy, so if you're going through a bad breakup or a parent just passed away, you may not be in the right frame of mind to make good decisions. It might make sense to wait a bit until things settle down.

You want to be going through this process with a clear head, making informed — not emotional — decisions, and not acting out of fear. If this is something you struggle with, a good habit to pick up is meditation. If you've never tried it, download an app like *Calm* or *Headspace* and go through their free trial, which is only a few minutes a day for a week.

2) Physical well-being

Leaving your job and starting a new gig can be stressful, and requires a lot of energy. There will be times during the process when you'll be juggling your day job and your side hustle at the same time, so you want to be operating at peak efficiency.

Want to know how entrepreneur Richard Branson oversees more than 400 companies? His number one productivity tip is working out. Meanwhile, entrepreneur Arianna Huffington's transformative secret weapon is getting enough sleep every night.

Here's a tip. Most people choose a quit date about six months out. This is the perfect opportunity to pair a commitment to joining a gym, exercising consistently, getting enough sleep, and eating right along with your career goal. Think of how amazing it will be to not only launch your dream career but also be healthier and happier when that day arrives.

3) Support system

Before starting your quest, make sure you have the support of those around you. This book is designed to teach you how to do things the right way, and while it might not be perfect, I think most can agree that surprising your partner by saying, "Guess what honey? I know we haven't talked about it at all, but I quit my job today! Um, can I borrow $20?"

As you go through the process, it's important to have the support of your family, your friends, and also a network of colleagues that you can rely on.

However, there's a big caveat here — not everyone is going to agree with what you're doing. Quitting a "good job" with "good benefits" and going out on your own is seen as incredibly risky by some, and they're going to do their best to tell you about all the ways you might fail.

You'll often have co-workers that try and drag you down like a drowning swimmer. Not only do they not want to see you leave the company, but often they're projecting their own fear of having a dead-end job, and if you leave, it highlights the fact that they're stuck too. Haters gonna hate.

So as you tell people about your plans, it's ok to listen to their well-intentioned advice. Just make sure to be selective of what you listen to, and also surround yourself with other people that have a positive outlook.

OK, so you've got your financial and emotional well-being set. Let's choose a date to quit.

Chapter 6: Choose Your Quit Date

With the necessary work of planning complete, in this chapter we're going to do something cool: choose the date that you're going to walk into your boss' office and quit your job. Remember, a goal is a dream with a deadline.

While other books might only focus on a specific calendar timeline for quitting, such as 90 days or 6 months, those figures don't focus on other factors that play a part for your individual situation. Here, we'll give you multiple considerations when planning your exit.

1) Monthly Timeline
No matter how desperate you are to leave, you want to give yourself enough time to prepare.

Take a look at your finances and determine how long it's going to take you to save up enough money to feel comfortable if it takes longer than you think to replace your income.

However, you don't want a runway so long that the date loses its urgency. If you say that you're going to quit two years from now, there's really not much incentive to buckle down and make things happen. With a multi-year window, it's always easy to push things off another month.

In the coming chapters, you'll be doing research to find out what the next stage of your career is going to look like. If it involves additional training and time to ramp up your skills in a new field, your timeline will be longer. If it's a matter of transitioning some existing consulting jobs into your new full-time venture, the window can be shorter.

If you're looking for a rule of thumb, a good range would be between 3 months and one year.

2) End of Lease Timeline
If changing your physical location by moving to a city with better opportunities or a lower cost of living is a

factor during your transition, then setting up a "end of lease" timeline might be the way to go.

Co-author Jim gives you a personal example:
It's easy to remember my wake-up call date because it's probably the most popular one out there — New Year's Day.

Despite the cold and snow and lingering hangover, I remember going for a run on January 1, 1998, and deciding it was time for me to quit my job. While my current job at a Boston tech startup wasn't terrible, there were three reasons I needed to leave:

1. I wanted to move to a different city
2. I wanted a job with an internet company
3. I wanted to pursue a job in sports

At first, I tried to determine how long I would need to make this transition. Six months? Nine months? A year? But as my run continued, the answer became obvious. My lease was up at the end of August — exactly eight full months away.

That timeframe seemed the perfect amount of time to learn new skills, create an online portfolio, and conduct a nationwide job search. I vowed that no matter what happened, I would not renew my lease.

The result? In early August I accepted a job and gave my notice, and on August 23rd I signed a new lease in Seattle, Washington.

So since a lease is often difficult to get out of, if your new venture is in a new location, basing your quit date around the expiration of a lease can be great timing.

3) Financial Timeline

Another way to time your exit is around a financial event. Looking back at our budget exercise, you can choose your quit date based on the date that you predict you'll have debts paid off and enough money in the bank. Or it could be the benchmark when the amount of revenue you're making in your side gig surpasses the amount you're making in your full-time job.

In some cases, the financial incentive will be driven by an event at your current day job. For example, many people have positions that pay out a bonus at the end of a quarter or end of the year. So if you're getting the itch to leave over the summer but want to wait until you receive your year-end bonus, that gives you about 6-8 months of planning before that check is in your hands. As another example, you might you have stock options that vest after a certain period.

4) Family Timeline

A fourth consideration might be timing your venture around a family event. Maybe you're living in a college town, and your partner is completing their Masters' degree in May. The plan might be for you to hang onto your job until they graduate, then launch your business once you're settled in a new location.

Or maybe you're having a baby in the near future. You might time things to stay at your corporate job while you still have full medical benefits, then pursue a work-remote job that is more conducive for a new parent.

5) Industry Timeline

A final way to pick your quit date is to time it based on your industry. For example, if you're a teacher, the logical time to make your exit is at the end of a school year.

Or perhaps your industry has traditionally slow and busy times. If you're a tax accountant, you might give yourself one more year of craziness and target a quit date of April 16 before heading to Hawaii to become a surfing instructor.

In co-author Jim's case, he built his quit day around an industry conference — or at least that was the plan:

I had been discontent in my job for some time, and after one particularly rough day in September, I stood up in my cubicle farm and said to no one in particular, "I think I'm going to quit my job next March."

My co-workers looked up from their desks, humored me, and said, "Why's that, Jim?" I told them that my side business was really picking up, and the annual SXSW Interactive conference was in March. I figured that would give me the 6-month window I needed. I would either let the company pay for the trip one more time, fulfill my obligations there, and then quit, or, I would quit before then and be able to launch my new business and get new clients at the conference.

In the end, things worked out, although not in the way that I planned. On November 1 of that year, I got laid off — and was thrilled. So while I didn't get the satisfaction of quitting, I did get a nice severance package and was forced to start my new gig sooner than later.

And as if destined by the career gods, the very first email I received after the layoff notification was from SXSW telling me that I had been chosen to speak and that I would receive a free Platinum level badge. I had made $1,000 in my first 5 minutes of being an entrepreneur!

This concludes Step 2, which has shown you the importance of having a plan, but crafting it to meet your needs and being willing to adapt. Take the time now to review your finances, your emotional state, and your timeline and mark your quit date on the calendar. Once you've done that, move on to Step 3, The (Fun) Research.

Step 3:
The (Fun) Research

Chapter 7: Four types of jobs

Welcome to Step 3, The Research. Or if you look more closely, we called it, the FUN research.

While you might think of "doing research" in your uninspiring corporate jobs or back in your college days as hard work, this really should be *fun*. Whether your new career is just a slight pivot or a completely new direction, you should be genuinely *excited* about it. After all, the entire goal of this process is to get out of a dreary job and find something that you're excited to do every morning. Kind of like the difference between researching information for your taxes vs. researching your next vacation.

Before we talk about finding what you want to do, let's

break down the four types of career moves you could consider, and how this book views each one.

1. Full-Time Job

The first type of transition is moving from a full-time job that you hate to a full-time job that you love. When you went through the "I hate my job because" exercise in Step 1, maybe you discovered that you just needed a new opportunity at a company with a better boss, a shorter commute, or higher pay. The key is to become keenly aware of what you want and what is fulfilling to you.

However, while there are certainly dream jobs and great companies out there that offer you flexibility and autonomy, you're still working for someone else and might find yourself in the same situation a year or so down the road when a new boss comes in or the company changes strategy. So for that reason, in this book, we're not going to focus so much on swapping one full-time job for another.

2. Full-scale Entrepreneurship

The second type of situation is what I'll call full-scale entrepreneurship; think Mark Zuckerberg with Facebook or Travis Kalanick of Uber.

While they generally share the same goals of independent consultants and business owners (creating something great, calling all the shots, and making a difference in the world), the distinction I want to make is that this type of person is looking to scale their business into a large, worldwide corporation.

That could mean raising venture capital, hiring hundreds or even thousands of employees, and having one of those cool offices that offer free lunch or uses scooters as the preferred method for getting from meeting to meeting.

Because there are so many complex elements that go into all of this, and essentially you're creating a new day job, we're going to focus on the next type of career.

3. Solopreneur

The third type of job is what is often referred to as being a Solopreneur. Here are the elements of that type of job:

- Company based around the unique skills of the owner
- Zero or few employees (usually contractors or virtual assistants)
- Often location independent

These jobs are often called "lifestyle businesses" because they place a premium on freedom and flexibility. You're able to do something you love, control the number of hours you work, and run your business from anywhere in the world. This is the type of work we'll focus on in the next lesson.

4. Hybrid model

But before we move on, I think it's worth noting that some people opt for a hybrid model.

- Some people reduce the number of days they work at their full-time job and run their business on the other days. As you'll see in the case studies, this is how author and entrepreneur Joanna Penn started out.

- Others essentially have two half jobs, one that's kind of mindless and pays the bills or offers health care; the other is their passion project. For example, you'll hear about my friend Naomi, who created a plan to work 20 hours a week in a structured job that she enjoys and offers benefits, while leaving the rest of the time to dedicate to her singing and teaching career.

- And finally, I'd be remiss if I (Jim) didn't mention my current situation. I am working full-time at Mirasee, which plays to my strengths of writing books, creating courses, leading a team, and sharing my knowledge to help other entrepreneurs succeed.

  However, the company not only allows — but encourages — our own side businesses, so I also have my own personal books, courses, and clients. And because we're a remote team, every employee has the freedom to work from anywhere and set their own hours.

  For example, our Operations Project Manager Maureen decided to leave the US and live and work remotely from around the world. As of this writing, she just finished up a stay in the Galapagos Islands, is touring other cities in Ecuador, and is prepping to head to Colombia and other destinations in South America. On more than one occasion, she literally dialed into our video team meetings from a hammock.

Takeaways

As you can see, the world of work has evolved into

several different models. To be clear, quitting your corporate gig and going out on your own doesn't mean automatic rainbows and butterflies. Sometimes entrepreneurship is glorified too much, only showing billionaire success stories on magazine covers, not the downsides of working alone or struggling in your business.

You'll also need to take on a lot more responsibility. As noted in the book *The E-Myth*, there's a difference between being a baker — making pastries — and running a bakery — doing accounting, marketing, sales, website development, design, and getting new customers. However, there are ways to streamline those tasks, and if you can make it all work, the rewards can far outweigh the costs.

Chapter 8: So what do you want to do?

When it comes to plotting out your next steps in life, people generally fall into one of three categories.

1. People that know *exactly* what they want to do
2. People that *kinda* know what they want to do
3. People that *have no idea* what they want to do

Let's address them one at a time.

1) People that know *exactly* what they want to do

There are many people that have a clear vision for what the day after their Quit Day will look like. Usually, these are people that have an established career and skill set, and make a smooth transition from the corporate world to the solopreneur world.

For example, you might be an *in-house designer* at an advertising agency, and know that you are going to leave to work with individual clients. Or you might be like my friend Alan, who'll you hear about later, who worked in one area of the transportation industry, and made a seamless transition into another segment of that same industry.

If this is your situation, your main goal at this stage is **execution**.

You won't be the first person to have done this, so your research should be around how others have succeeded in the past. Let's take the example of the designer going freelance.

What are the hallmarks of a successful freelance design business? More importantly, what are the main reasons that this type of business *fails*? Is it the quality of the work, not charging enough, or attracting new clients?

The focus of your research here should be networking with other successful business owners, finding a mentor, and setting up systems to ensure that your business will be profitable from the get-go. For example, my friend Marina runs a successful design business in Seattle. Here was the breakthrough that enabled her to truly scale:

"The single best thing I ever did for my business? I hired a bookkeeper/personal assistant. She makes sure my estimated taxes are on time, my licenses are updated, my business expenses are recorded, and that everything from receipts to creative ideas and sketches is filed correctly. Oh, and countless other things.

She's paid for herself numerous times over and allows me to do what I'm efficient at (great design), instead of spending time doing things I'm less good at and that I find easy to put off (like never-ending paperwork).

She comes to my house once a week, at a certain time, which keeps the hours low, because we can keep up on tasks. In this scheduled time I also do personal finances and make financial plans for the future. It makes my business run like clockwork."

2) People that *kinda* know what they want to do

The second category of people is those that have a pretty good idea what their next step is. They usually want to stay within the same industry or use the same skill set, but aren't quite sure what that will be or what the business will look like.

For this example, let's say you are a *copywriter* at an advertising agency. You know a few things: you love to write, you love business, and you love the nuances of persuasion and sales. Or you might be like my friend Andy, who'll you hear about later, who worked in one area of the creative marketing world and knew he wanted to stay in that realm, but wasn't sure how his solopreneur practice would look.

If this is your situation, your main goal at this stage is **evolution**.

This involves looking at your core strengths and figuring out the puzzle pieces for where you go next. How does your career evolve?

Let's take the example of the copywriter that wants to go out on their own. They should think about the intersection of their core skills: writing, business, and sales copy.

One avenue could be writing a series of business books about copywriting and self-publishing them on Amazon. Another avenue could be approaching large real estate companies and helping them with the sales copy for their printed sales brochures.

The key here is to dig deeper, continually asking questions and looking for the next evolution of what you love to do. For example, the copywriter might realize they thrive on writing short-form copy, not book-length projects. They might prefer to work with individuals, not large businesses. And as they look down the line, they think it's a much better strategy to focus on web-based writing, not print.

Thus, rather than some variation of the two options listed, the evolution of their skills might be to help single-person businesses write effective copy for their websites.

3) People that *have no idea* what they want to do

The last category of people is those that aren't sure what they're going to do after they quit, but it sure as heck isn't the thing they're doing now. Sometimes they build on their previous skills, but just as often they're ready for a total 180.

For this example, let's say you are an *account manager* at an advertising agency, and you're sick of it. You hate dealing with clients and their constant last-minute changes, which force you to work ungodly hours. You're not getting paid enough to live in a decent apartment, and you were just turned down in your request for a raise. You hate your boss and the cut-throat environment of advertising. Besides, you were a *psychology major* for the love of Pete. You're asking yourself, "How the heck did I end up here?" Or you might be like my friend Dan, the high school teacher that is ready to do something — anything — new, now that the initial reward he got from teaching has gone away.

If this is your situation, your main goal at this stage is **exploration.**

This involves a bit more work to figure out your next steps, but again, it should be fun. In this stage, it can often be helpful to take an "anything goes" attitude and list all the possible things you might enjoy doing, and then whittling them down as you explore and find out which elements (pay, hours, freedom, etc.) line up with your core values.

Later on, we'll explore the elements you need to launch a successful business and find the work you're meant to do.

Let's take the example of the account manager that wants to go out on their own.

They must have chosen psychology as a major for a reason, right? What initially attracted them to that subject? When they were in school, did they devour every research paper on the subject and excel at it, or did they approach their classes with dread? If they view business as cut-throat, what would the opposite of that look like? What are some "softer" occupations that focus on well-being and helping others? And if lifestyle is an issue, what is a field that lets you set your own hours, choose your own clients, work from anywhere, and make a good living — all without a boss?

The answers to those questions could lead the person to explore the possibility of becoming a life coach, which ticks off every box on that list, but there are dozens of other compatible fields that could play to their strengths as well.

No matter which bucket you fall into, it's important to gain clarity before you immerse yourself into your next career. Let's go deeper into discovering your craft.

Chapter 9: Should you follow your passion?

OK, so you're planning on quitting a job you hate, but you have no idea what you want to do next. Or maybe you have a pretty good idea, but you want to hone in further to make sure that you'll be a success. Without fail, during your research and discovery phase, someone is going to utter the following advice:

Follow Your Passion!

It's obvious, right? Just follow your passion, and you'll be happy and successful.

It's advice that has been handed down for ages. Confucius once said, "Choose a job you love, and you will never have to work a day in your life." But life can be a little more complicated.

When I was 23, I was working for a software company near Boston, and they announced they were moving the entire department to Atlanta.

They were really good about it, giving us about a month's notice, letting us leave the office at any time to go on interviews, and offering us a small budget for job search expenses.

With that money I bought a book called, "Do What You Love and the Money Will Follow." As a young professional with exactly 18 months of work experience, it sounded like pretty good advice to me. As I look back over my 20+ year career, I truly took it to heart:

- I was passionate about sports, so I got a job at one of the world's leading sports companies.

- I was passionate about technology, so I got a job at one of the world's leading tech publications.

- And I was passionate about career development, so I wrote a book on the subject, mentored young professionals, and offered career consulting services.

Piece of cake, right?

Oh if it were only that easy.

While the concept of the book is inspirational, what people tend to overlook is the hard work that needed to be done to make those dreams a reality.

- Months of research, job searching, and networking just to get my foot in the door.

- Preparing for weeks on end to make sure the 3,000-mile journey for the one shot at an interview would not be in vain.

- Blogging thousands of words for years – for free – before even thinking about writing a book.

Let's look how things have changed.

Follow Your Passion?

Smash cut to the present day, and the advice is a bit different. Few people are quoting Confucius, and career advice from the 1990s is about as relevant as the Motorola StarTAC flip phone (although trust me, kids, it sold 60 million units and was the epitome of cool).

In fact, so many people have been preaching "Follow your passion!" lately, that there's been a backlash, to the point where it's now cool to tell people NOT to follow their passion.

Let's take a look at some of the Google results for that phrase:

- To Find Work You Love, Don't Follow Your Passion
- Follow Your Passion Is Crappy Advice
- Why "Follow Your Passion" is Pretty Bad Advice
- Is 'Follow Your Passion' A Good Idea Or Dumb Advice?
- The Many, Many Problems With Follow Your Passion
- Cal Newport: Follow Your Passion Is Bad Advice
- The Secrets To Career Contentment: Don't Follow Your Passion
- Why Follow Your Passion Is Awful, Flawed Advice

Wow. So which is it?

I know a lot of people fear turning their hobby into a job, and I get that. For example, I really enjoy going to the gym a few days a week. But that doesn't mean I want to turn it into a job as a personal trainer and spend

8 hours a day, 5 days a week at the gym trying to hustle clients. There's a line between *wanting* to do something you enjoy, and *having* to do something you enjoy.

Best-selling author Cal Newport argues that, instead of viewing passion as a starting point, you should look at it as something that is gained over time by finding out what you're good at, what you like to do, and what you don't like to do. Rather than *following* your passion, you *cultivate* it.

He says that "mastering a rare and valuable skill is the key to generating a remarkable life." In other words, follow the advice of Steve Martin, who said, "Be so good they can't ignore you."

Let's look at a framework to help you out.

Chapter 10: Discovering your career

So if following your passion isn't enough, what else is needed? Rather than just blindly following your heart, it's helpful to add some logic.

The goal is to make sure you're taking several factors into consideration, not just blindly following your heart, but also exploring the business implications.

A useful framework is the Japanese concept of Ikigai, a Venn diagram that explores four areas of your career:

Your Career: Venn Diagram
What you love
What you're good at
What you can be paid for

What the world needs

Graphic representation by @emmyzen (Emmy van Deurzen) via Creative Commons

As you execute on your vision, evolve your skills, and explore your next steps, run your ideas through each of the parts of the Venn diagram.

To use my example, my passions are sports, technology, and career development. Those are the *things I love*.

But to get the job at ESPN, I had to *be good at my job* as a technical producer. Considering more than 100 million people watch the Super Bowl each year, it's safe to say there are a LOT of sports fans out there, and a lot of them would love to work in sports. But if they don't have a skill that is in demand to go along with that passion, they won't be considered.

To get a job in technology, again, passion was a given. But because I was coming in with 15 years of digital marketing experience, it was *something I could be paid for*.

And to be able to get paying clients for my own business, I needed to offer *something the world needed*, such as helping others learn how to negotiate so that they could get paid more. See how it all ties together?

To get you started and hone in on *your* Ikigai, here are a few questions you can ask yourself:

- What topic do people come to you for, when looking for help or advice?

For example, without even thinking, if you were to write to me and say, "I need some help with sales," I'd send you to my friend Bobby. If you said, "I need advice on Facebook marketing," I'd send you to my friend Helen. And if you said, "I need to know where the best burger in New York is," I'd send you to my friend Phil.

I make these associations instantly, which is important because it means they've built up that skill as part of their brand, giving them a word-of-mouth marketing advantage. If you don't know what your specialty is, ask your friends and family.

- How would you spend your time if you were a multi-millionaire and didn't have to work?

While it's key to factor revenue into the picture, this question helps you brainstorm opportunities by freeing up your mind to think of the possibilities if money wasn't a factor.

While it's easy to say you would lay on the beach, travel the world, or "do nothing," take it seriously. Once you've bought your Ferrari and been to Paris several times, how would you spend your days? What are the first few things that come to mind?

- During what activities do you find yourself in "flow?"

Flow is a state where you're effortlessly in the zone doing something you love, so much that you'll often not notice time flying by. Have you ever been editing vacation videos, creating a website, or talking to a friend about a project you're working on, look up and say, "Whoa, where did the last 2 hours go?"

Historical sources hint that Michelangelo may have painted the ceiling of the Vatican's Sistine Chapel while in a flow state. It is reported that he painted for days at a time, and he was so absorbed in his work that he did not stop for food or sleep until he reached the point of passing out. He would wake up refreshed and, upon starting to paint again, re-entered a state of complete absorption.

Start to pay attention to those times in your life. Solopreneurship is great when it's going well, but it also needs to be something you can focus on for hours on end when things need improvement.

Take some time to list out career paths that fit into the Ikigai framework. Once you're done, advance to the next chapter, where we'll take the concept a step further, and add a few modern elements.

Chapter 11: Defining your craft

While you've most likely seen some form of the career Venn diagram before, and the concept of Ikigai has probably been around for a long time, the idea of what a career is has changed along with the new economy we live in.

The new economy:

- No longer do people stay in the same job for years on end

- Cubicle farms have started to give way to coworking spaces and ergonomic workstations

- Technology allows us to work from anywhere and attract clients worldwide

- More people are searching for the larger meaning in what they do

At the same time, there's something amazing when you find someone that has truly mastered their craft. Sure it can be great if you're an engineer and jumped from Microsoft to Facebook to Uber to some hot flying startup we haven't even heard of yet.

But what about Jacob Ferrato, a custom sneaker creator who hand sews just 75 pairs per year from his warehouse, charging anywhere from $1,000 to $2,500 or more. As profiled in *WIRED*, he only sources one type of Italian-made soles, employs four different sewing machines, and favors old school Japanese and European knives for handcrafting the leather. Only in his mid-20s, this is someone who seems to have already *mastered his craft*.

Your Craft: Zen Diagram

In acknowledging the changing factors of the new economy, I was on a panel with three other friends — Helen Todd, Jey Van-Sharp, and Adam Marelli — and we expanded on the traditional Venn Diagram and called it the Zen Diagram.

During our discussion, we talked about not just what it meant to have a career, but what it truly meant to overcome fear and develop a craft — finding your life's purpose.

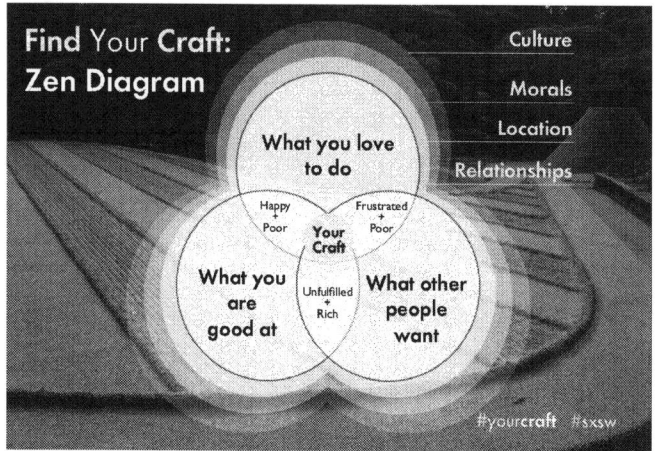

Image by Jim Hopkinson, Helen Todd, Jey Van-Sharp, Adam Marelli

So beyond the three elements of what you love to do, what other people want, and what you're good at, we added four additional considerations:

1) Culture

The first element is culture. Working at a high-flying mobile startup is a lot different than an established brick and mortar corporation. Culture matters. When you're launching your new gig, think about what the culture means to you, even if you're a one-man shop.

Do you want to be known as hip and cool and trendy, or rock-solid and trustworthy? Are you showing up to client meetings in jeans and a hoodie, or do you prefer a fashionable button-down and a bow tie? Do you pride yourself on transparency? Diversity? Bleeding edge technology?

2) Morals

More and more individuals — especially millennials — are using the phrase "I want to make a difference in the world" when thinking of their career and their craft. Companies like TOMS Shoes and Warby Parker have proven that not only can you run a solid business, but you can also make giving back a cornerstone of your company.

What morals will you infuse into the company you create? Are you a proudly female-owned business that will volunteer to help other women start their own companies? Will you give a portion of every sale to charity? Do you refuse to work with companies tied to poor working conditions for overseas workers? In short, what do you stand for?

3) Location

Now more than ever, the internet has made it possible to work from anywhere. What does that mean for you? Will you join the growing trend of city-based living, with the energy, conveniences, and transportation options that come with it? Or is your goal to flee the hectic chaos of the urban environment, and work quietly from a remote mountain retreat?

In the past, "the what people want" segment was a much larger factor. Certain industries simply required you to live in a certain part of the world. If what you were good at and loved doing was car manufacturing, then the companies that wanted that and were willing to pay you for that were probably at a factory in Detroit. Today, while it might be crucial for your job to be near certain customers, if you're designing your next career and location independence is important to you, you must use that consideration.

4) Relationships

One factor we noticed was not included in the original diagram was relationships. This could cover the following:

- Spouse
- Children
- Parents
- Family members
- Friends
- Business partners

- Network
- Clients

Any of these relationships could be crucial to your long-term business success and happiness, so think about what's important to you. It could be good schools for your children, being close to an aging parent, or staying close to a network of like-minded professionals.

As you can see, there are a lot of factors to consider in the modern career. I can't see many millennials saying, "I've decided to move to Naples, Florida because a Forbes.com slideshow showed that it had the top projected annual job growth increase, 4.6%!"

Rather, people will consider a much wider array of options that incorporate their culture, morals, and relationships. Let's continue with our research.

Chapter 12: The real research

Quitting your job and setting out on your own is all about balance. The reason you're probably here is that your wake-up call threw you significantly out of balance. You just couldn't take it anymore from your boss, your commute, your paycheck, or your work.

We've covered the balance between your financial inventory and your emotional state. We've analyzed the elements of a career, as well as your craft. We've talked about following your passion, but also looking at what you can get paid for.

Let's continue moving forward with that balance, a reality check on your business viability.

By now, you've probably brainstormed some dream careers:

"I want to become a productivity blogger and work from a villa in Tuscany!"

"I want to write thriller novels that are Amazon bestsellers!"

"I love to cook! I should become a chef like on TV!"

"I want to open a quaint coffee shop in New York that serves Vienna roast… from Vienna!"

"I want to create an app that helps the Chinese market understand mobile advertising!"

"I want to start my own SAAS software company and get recurring income every month!"

"Uh, hold on. I still have no idea what I want to do. Please help me!"

The truth is, if you really want to do any of those jobs, you can. But there are real costs to each of them. And when you do the real research, you'll find out. Let's break down all 7 of them and see what we find.

"I want to become a productivity blogger and work from a villa in Tuscany!"

Ah, the dream of passive income. All it takes is one glance at the income reports on Pat Flynn's *Smart*

Passive Income blog to spur the desire to work remotely from a beach. Pat has made more than $50,000 per month, every month, since 2013, and in 2016 cracked $150,000 in each of the first four months.

But here's the thing. It isn't just a dream. Not only is he doing it, but he's also showing you exactly how he's doing it, including the $40,000 in *expenses* every month.

That doesn't mean it's going to be easy. In fact, most beginning bloggers would be best served at even shooting for $50,000 per year, let alone per month.

The good news is, some online entrepreneurs are nice enough to "open up the kimono" and show you what really goes into a business, so you're not just dreaming, you're seeing the expenses behind the scenes.

Check out the site Cash Flow Diaries (cashflowdiaries.com), where they've published *The Ultimate List of Monthly Blogger Income Reports*. You'll usually see Pat Flynn at the top, but it's a great reality check to see the bloggers making just $1,000 or even $50 per month. We all have to start somewhere.

"I want to write thriller novels that are Amazon bestsellers!"

Think you just need to start writing and hit publish? Check out the case study of Joanna Penn, and how she went from IT professional to a single book, to being an award-winning, New York Times best-selling author, selling 450,000 books in 74 countries and five languages. Her story proves that it's possible, but it also shows the reality of time invested and the work involved.

"I love to cook! I should become a chef like on TV!"

If there's any profession that is the poster child for the disconnect between doing what you love and designing a dream career, I think it's chef. Just because you love whipping up a lasagna or a tarragon salmon dish once in awhile — while listening to an NPR podcast and casually sipping some Pinot Noir — does not mean you should quit your job and become a cook.

In Step 4, we're going to talk about testing out your new career before jumping in. But in this case, just one conversation might be enough to persuade you.

When I asked my friend Matt, a master-level chef with 20+ years of experience, about what the experience is like, he told me, "The hours are long, the work is stressful, it's certainly not always fun, and it can actually be quite dangerous since everything in the kitchen is HHSS."

After giving him a confused look, he replied, "Hot, Heavy, Slippery, or Sharp."

"I want to open a quaint coffee shop in New York that serves Vienna roast from Vienna!"

If you're looking for a close runner up that shows why you need to focus on the reality, not the dream, check out the article on Slate titled, *Bitter Brew: I opened a charming neighborhood coffee shop. Then it destroyed my life.* (Remember, all links in the book can be found at http://mrse.co/quit-your-job-links).

"I want to create an app that helps the Chinese market understand mobile advertising!"

This might seem like a strange example, but here's why I chose it.

Once again I want to highlight the disparity between the dream and the costs. Back in April 2011 when my book came out, it was less than a year from the launch of the Apple iPad and apps were all the rage. I was incredibly excited about designing and launching a companion app to go along with my book.

There were just two problems: First, the price that people were paying for apps was going down. A huge majority of the items in the app store were free, and according to some research I had pulled, nearly half of the paid apps were priced at just 99 cents (with Apple taking a 30% cut).

Second, the cost of app development was going up. I was in talks with one mobile developer and in the span of two weeks, he nearly doubled his price since he had so many clients coming in. Back then, I think the cost to develop a pretty straightforward app was about $10,000, but today unless you're a programmer yourself, you might pay $25,000 to $50,000 or more depending on complexity. That's a lot of downloads at 99 cents if you want to make your money back.

But the other reason I want to highlight this is that I was looking at big picture trends. In 2010, I would have been betting that the app ecosystem was going to continue to grow.

Looking at data from statista.com, my hunch was right. The number of downloaded apps grew from 4 billion to 130 billion! Shoot, maybe I should have made that app anyway.

One of my favorite resources for emerging trends is Mary Meeker's annual internet trends report, which can be found at kpcb.com/internet-trends.

So if you DO have some expertise in the China market, and you see a chart that shows growth in the past 6 years is the same as the previous 30 combined (slide 24 of her 2016 report), and you DO have experience in mobile advertising and see that there's a $22 billion opportunity in that space (slide 45), then that's the kind of data you need to move forward with confidence.

"I want to start my own SAAS software company and get recurring income every month!"
Here's a final example of doing the real research. Perhaps you want to create a SAAS product — software as a service — that gives you recurring revenue every month.

If you dig around, you can find sample numbers. Amy Hoy published a post literally called, "5 Years of SaaS Growth: Every Month, Exact Numbers." The simple takeaway: Yes it can be done, no it can't be done overnight.

An even better article is by Nathan Barry, the solopreneur founder of email company ConvertKit. One of his articles (nathanbarry.com/5k/) shows how he grew the company from $0 to $5,000 in recurring revenue per month.

Better still is his update (nathanbarry.com/30k/) showing how he grew the company from that $5,000 a month to $30,000 per month.

If you have a chance to check it out, the graph within it is beautiful… the standard "hockey stick" line of growth. But make sure you notice the two years where growth was mostly stagnant. Now do you know why we emphasized having plenty of money in the bank back in Step 2?

But before you move on, you actually have to *read* the article, not just look at the pretty growth charts. If you do, you'll get to the section titled, "So how much is profit?" Let me focus on three quotes:

"I get this question all the time. Even back when we were doing $5,000/month people would ask what our profit was. Turns out $-8,000/month wasn't the answer they were expecting."

"Out of our $30,000/month in revenue that we have today, none of it is profit. We're still growing, and I spend almost every dollar as it comes in."

"I pay myself a very small salary ($3,000/month) which combined with a little money from book and course sales covers my expenses."

So how does this story end? While it's tough to predict the future, as we published the book in mid-2016, Nathan released yet another article (nathanbarry.com/profit/) showing an incredible 10x increase to more than $300,000 per month in recurring revenue.

Once again, while it's great to look at the growth, this time around he focuses on yet another set of critical elements for building a real business: focusing on profit margins, cutting costs, getting efficient, reinvestments, and sacrifice.

The point of this chapter is that the information you need is out there if you look hard enough. Yes, inspiration is key. But you're a fool if you don't dig into the hard numbers of what makes a successful business tick.

"Uh, hold on. I still have no idea what I want to do. Please help me!"

Oh wait, what about the people that are still unsure? If you've done the soul searching and analyzed your skills, yet you're no closer to knowing what you want, one recommendation is to hire a coach.

There are plenty of amazing career coaches out there that are trained to draw out your innate skills and help you explore careers that will be a good match for you.

So how much time should you spend researching? I have a helpful graph in the next chapter.

Chapter 13: How much to research

Now that you've seen the importance of research, how long should you spend researching? Guess what? Once again, it's a balance.

Luckily I've created this handy graph to help you out:

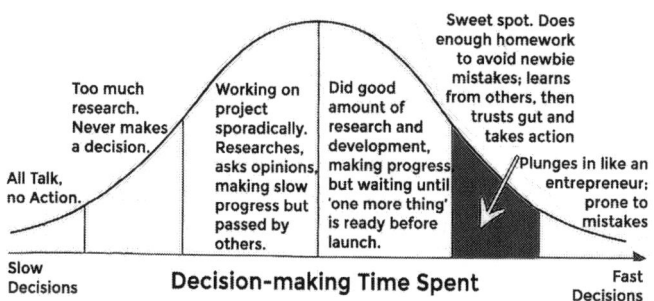

Graphic by Jim Hopkinson

- First, on the far left, are the people that are all talk, no action. They're the ones in the break room talking about their dream, but they never explore it.

- Then there are the endless researchers. To them, looking into their dream feels like they're doing something. They spend weeks, months, or even years saying they are going to do something, but don't.

- Next are the people that research all the different ways that others have done something, from launching a website to starting a business to traveling the world. Maybe they take an online course or two. Or ten. Or twenty. They might try a few projects, but ultimately wait too long and are passed by others.

- The next set of people do all the right research and even are ready to launch or make a change in their life. However, fear and perfectionism hold them back as they wait for the moment that everything is perfect, which of course it never will be. In the saddest cases, it's a life that leads to regret.

- Now let's jump to the far right, where you'll find people that are too impulsive. They leap into the latest and greatest venture without thinking things through. They blow time and money on one project after another, never stopping to wonder if what they're working on is a good fit for them.

These are the people that decide to become a chef or open a coffee shop or build an app on a whim, only realizing the true realities after it's too late. Sometimes they never stick with a project long enough to see it through, jumping to the next new thing once they get bored or hit the first roadblock.

And quite often, they exert twice the time and effort reinventing the wheel, when a little advice from mentors that have been there before and made newbie mistakes would have let them get to their goals faster.

So what's the sweet spot? I call it Observe with Intent, Act with Purpose.

Observe With Intent

When you have an idea, whether it's moving to Japan or quitting your job and launching your own design firm, it benefits you to do the research first.

In almost every case, there is going to be someone before you that has done the same thing, and you can benefit greatly from not making the same mistakes they did. You want to become educated enough that you don't look back and realize you made a stupid, newbie mistake.

- Research and read up on the subject
- Take some courses and read the best books on the subject
- Talk to trusted friends, and even solicit advice from strangers
- Know what you're getting into
- Make sure your excitement about it is genuine
- Learn about best practices

Then stop there, trust your gut, and go for it. You're in the sweet spot.

Act With Purpose

Then, act with purpose. Take specific, deliberate, actionable steps to test your ideas:

- Create a simple website about your idea and ask people for their email address to get more information

- Pick up the phone and talk to potential clients – and ask for the sale
- Write that first blog post or film that first video – then click publish

If you find you're doing any of the following, you're in danger of paralyzing yourself with inaction:

- You want to check with EVERYONE before you make a decision

- You want to take one more course, read one more book, or check one more email

- You start basing too many decisions on data only and not listening to your heart

- You start getting conflicting information from people, blurring your ability to see your original plan

- You start listening to naysayers and negative people, who start doubting you or listing all the ways your idea won't succeed

- You tell yourself you'll move forward when the exact time is right

Like anything in life, your individual personality will dictate exactly where you fall along the scale. Once again, we're back to the concept of balance.

But as you sketch out your plan, try and stay aware of our advice and note where you are along the scale of "too much research" vs. "too impulsive." Observe with intent, act with purpose.

Following our own advice, the research phase is now over. It's time to take action.

Step 4:
Hustle and Flow

Chapter 14: Finding the time

Our creeping rollercoaster climb of research has reached its apex, so pause and look around at the corporate landscape one final time. You're now ready to start taking action, embarking on the stomach-tingling thrill of solopreneurship.

While the ride will certainly be exciting, with lots of twists and turns and ups and downs, that doesn't mean it has to be unsafe and risky.

Plain and simple, one of the safest ways to enjoy the ride is to start developing your business on the side, putting in the hours and doing the extra work while you're still at your full-time job.

OK. Now I'm going to sit back and wait for the excuses to come in.

Let me guess… You're already working too much at your current job. You don't have time. There aren't enough hours in the day. You're already exhausted.

I don't want to hear it.

First of all, you hate your job, remember? Channel that hatred and think about how amazing it's going to feel on quitting day.

Second, you're transitioning to something you love, right? If you can't get motivated to work on this stuff on the side, then you should probably go back to Step 3 and find something that you *are* excited enough to work on.

I understand this can be a challenge, so let's address it up front and offer some suggestions.

- Cut out television
The average American still watches more than 5 hours of TV a day. If you're one of them, that's a whopping 30 or 40 hours a week freed up for your business.

Do you watch the news for 30 minutes every night? The 5-day weather forecast and final score of tonight's game is just a 10-second tap away on an app, and the negative news and violence probably isn't the best thing to end your night with (if you must stay up on current events, download an app like *NY Times Now*, which lets you swipe through the top few stories in a minute or two).

What about sitcoms and movies and dramas with dragons? Think back about that tombstone. It's your choice.

Here lies Thomas, he…

A) Started his own business and lived a full and happy life
B) Didn't miss a single episode of *The Big Bang Theory* and never revealed a spoiler on *Game of Thrones*

- **Cut social media**
Facebook. Twitter. Reddit. Instagram. Every minute you spend on these sites is a minute not working on your business. Go on a social media hiatus for a month or two and think about how awesome it will be to go back on — and announce your new venture.

Here, I'll even let you know what you missed in advance: Your co-worker with the cute baby posted cute baby pictures. Your well-off cousin is #blessed to be traveling first class to Antigua. That fringe friend from high school is talking fringe politics again. OMG did you see what that cat just did? And — shocker! — that too-perfect couple that calls each other "schmoopie" wasn't really that perfect. #divorce

- Stay up late

I know a lot of people have kids, which is a full-time job in itself. It's ok. Send them off with a good breakfast. Pick them up at the bus stop. Make sure to spend quality time at dinner. Help them with their homework.

Tuck them into bed and tell them a scary story about a wicked troll that lives under a bridge named Conrad. Lie and wrap up the story when they say, "Wait, Daddy, isn't that the name of your boss?"

Then go downstairs, get on the computer, and put in a few hours of work. If that sounds ambitious, start with just 30 minutes per night, and build on it. But get started.

- Get up early

Same deal. Carve out an extra hour or two by getting up at 5 am during the week or 7 am on a weekend. Yes, you might have to live on 5-6 hours of sleep instead of 7-8 for a few months. But they've actually done extensive studies on millions of people that have been able to function on limited sleep for months on end. They're called *new parents*.

The point is this. Did you brush your teeth this morning? Geesh, I thought you were so busy! How did you find the time? The truth is, if it's important to you, you'll find the time. Make it a priority.

Chapter 15: Take a test drive

With enough research under our belts to make an informed decision and a commitment to making the time, you're ready to take action.

While there are many ways to make the transition, our recommendation is to try out your new business idea on the side while you're still at your full-time job — commonly known as a side hustle.

Ben Fanning is a Burnout Specialist who helps frustrated professionals rekindle their passion for the job. He says that quitting your job without tasting the freedom of what your next gig will be like first is like:

- Marrying someone you've never met
- Buying a car without test driving it

- Purchasing a house without going inside first

For a job such as freelance design, you might already be way ahead of the game. Chances are, you've probably used your personal time to help a friend (or even a paying client) design a logo or build a website while you were still at your full-time job. Now is the time to "go pro" and turn these one-off side projects into a real business, so focus on building out a client roster of paying customers.

For writer Joanna Penn, it all started with writing a single book. She didn't start out intending to author multiple series of books that would become best sellers. She just wrote one book and got it out there to the world.

For Alan, it was securing one client in the shipping industry that he knew he could help. Then another. Then another.

But no matter what, it's important to *experience* what your new venture will be like before you go all in.

There are a few ways to do this:

- In some cases, you can just jump in and start. Take the example of Tom, an avid mountain biker and hiker who constantly found himself coming back to the beautiful small town of Jim Thorpe, Pennsylvania. For five years, he and his friends built up insider knowledge of all the intricate trails in the area. When he and his wife finally moved there for good in 2002, a business — the Jim Thorpe Experience — was born.

He didn't have to invest in infrastructure or worry about whether to form an LLC or an S Corporation. He just saw a space where there was something he loved and was good at — biking and hiking — and something that had a demand that people would pay for — guided tours of the area to make the most of their vacation.

- If it's something a bit more ambitious, consider taking a class. Thinking about being a teacher? Rather than dropping $50,000 on a Masters in Education, how about testing out a single Professional Studies class for a few hundred dollars?

- If you really do think your calling is being a chef, that's easy. Take a part-time job working in a kitchen.

- In many cases, you can volunteer. This doesn't mean you are doomed to work for free forever, but if you can't handle working 10 or 20 hours a week for a few months in your supposed dream profession to gain experience, then you won't make it when you're doing it for real.

- Another important factor is to get to that first sale. Sign that first client. Bring in that first dollar. Kind of like the Greek restaurant on the corner that has an old dollar from 1971 taped to the wall. The guys on the *Internet Business Mastery* podcast call this the "Money Milestone," and it's significant. Even if it's just a few dollars from your first ebook, that magical Paypal deposit from the sale of a course, or getting paid $100 to speak to a small group, it means something.

All of this sounds obvious, but for some people, it's not. It's as if they're waiting for permission to be told it's allowed.

I experienced this first-hand while volunteering at a career event.

A young man came up to me and told me that his goal was to be a writer or editor. So my next question was excitedly saying, "Great! I'm a writer as well. So... do you have a website? Are you blogging? What are you writing about right now?" I was caught off guard to hear that he was doing *none* of those things.

Then a woman told me she really loved event planning. That was *definitely* the type of job she wanted. So I said, "Very cool! I actually run a little conference on the side myself; it's a blast. What about you? I'm guessing you're the person that organizes trips for all your friends, right? Do you have any events that you run now? Do you have a book club or meetup group or networking happy hour that you put together on a regular basis?" Once again, the person got uncomfortable and stared down at her shoes without an answer.

Lastly, I found myself speaking with a talkative, confident, well-dressed woman. She said her dream was to work for a media company and some day be an on-air personality. You can see where this is going. I thought she'd be perfect for that role, so I held my breath and asked, "So, are you doing anything like that now? You must have a YouTube channel or a podcast or constantly be making quick videos on your phone and posting them on Facebook, right? Or wait, are you using any of the new live streaming apps? Taking improv classes? Some other creative outlet to share your personality? Yes?" The answer, sadly, was no. Strike 3.

My takeaway couldn't be more obvious.

If you want to be a writer, you should be writing. A lot.
If you want to be on camera, you should be making videos.
If you want to work in event planning, plan some events.
If you want to work at a non-profit and give back, volunteer.
If you want to be a designer, you should have a website, a portfolio, and have so many designs that you've done in the past six months that it's painful to select just a few of the best to display.

This experience ties back nicely to Cal Newport's research. You don't develop a passion by *dreaming*; you develop it by *doing*.

We'll look at another example of this in the next chapter, as we dig even deeper into the nature of passion and what it takes to create your ideal career.

Chapter 16: The case of true passion

One of the challenges you might be facing as you progress through this process is the question, "How can I tell if I'm passionate enough about something to invest in it as a new career?"

Running through the elements of the Zen Diagram in Chapter 11 gives you a good framework, and it's pretty easy to recognize at a surface level if you're generally enjoying something as you do it, but let's continue to dig deeper and ask questions.

A few years back I wrote an article for *Salary.com* about a great thread on *reddit.com* that ties in with this topic.

A man wrote in to say he was having a heated debate with his wife. They had worked hard, saved well, and promised to pay for their daughter's college education. His daughter was now looking at schools and announced that she wanted to pursue a film degree.

His concern was that they would be paying $60,000-$70,000 toward a major where she'd have an extremely hard time getting employed. He genuinely wanted the best for his daughter, but didn't want her to think they'd simply take care of her if things don't work out.

He also wanted to be on the same page with his wife, who said she'd be livid if he refused to front the money for their daughter's education. What should he do?

The comments that ensued were both insightful and passionate:

- Some focused on the ridiculous cost of education these days
- Some said that he needed to keep his promise to his daughter no matter what
- Some said he had every right to give input since it was his money

A debate grew between those advocating, "follow your passion" vs. "be realistic."

However, I thought the best piece of advice was from the user "stibera," a college counselor at an art school that took the time to reply with a 1,000-word response, echoing the main theme people had brought up, which was:

"Does your daughter show a true passion for film?"

He asked, "Has your daughter made any of her own films? Is she expressing strong interest in the technology and philosophies around filmmaking? Does she watch films and show a desire to want to understand its history?"

In other words,

- Does she watch films whenever she can, not as an ordinary teenager, but with a director's eye and appreciation?

- Does she have her own video camera and gear?

- Does she care about things like audio quality and lighting?

- Is she spending every weekend creating short films, honing her work, and showing that creativity on YouTube?

- Is she a film nerd, constantly quoting from movies and pointing out script inconsistencies in bad romantic comedies?

- Does she have a strong opinion between lav mics and shotgun mics?

If *that* was why she wanted to be a film major, then he could feel a lot better about her choice of major. If she was choosing film because "it seems cool" or she "likes going to movies," he should think twice.

The college counselor's suggestion and advice:

"If she's just interested in putzing around with a camera, spend $6,000 — not $60,000 — and buy her a nice camera, let her take a gap year, and travel and play around with her fancy new technology. She'll figure it out one way or the other that way. If she's an engaged child who shows a passion for film, when the year is over, a $60,000 investment in the right film school could help launch a successful career for her."

User "StegasaurusTom" added, "It's win/win/win. If she bums around and wastes the opportunity, then she has no one to blame but herself and you don't waste your money. If she really takes advantage of it, then she'll have a great experience and even more passion. Ultimately this puts the ball in her court and I'd be willing to bet that the majority of film/art students would have killed for this opportunity."

There are three takeaways here that relate to this book:

1. Good news! You're an adult! You don't need your parent's permission to pursue your next project.

2. When exploring your options, invest the smallest amount possible to determine if the next step is right for you.

3. If it's an idea you truly feel is worthwhile — not just something you think would be cool — you'll leap at the opportunity to learn more about it.

Personally, I love the idea of the travel year. Whether the person ends up becoming a famous film director or not isn't the point. No matter what, she'll likely come away with a portfolio of skills – how to take great photos, what makes for a compelling video, an editing style, storytelling techniques, and interpersonal skills that can be useful in any career. In the next chapter, we explore the importance of building out a portfolio of expertise.

Chapter 17: The portfolio career

One mainstay of the corporate world is the one-word job title. When someone asks, "What do you do?" there are many workers that can answer in a single word, often tied to their department or reminiscent of a college major: Accounting. Finance. Engineering. Sales.

On one hand, it can be advantageous to be known for one thing and only one thing. For example, my friend Gina has a solo business and does tax accounting for startups. Does she do tax accounting for *large corporations*? No, she does tax accounting for *startups*. Does she do growth hacking for startups? No, she does *tax accounting* for startups. Pretty clear. The upside is that if you're at an event and someone says, "I just launched a startup and need someone to do our taxes," you know who to call.

But just as "solopreneur" has entered our vocabulary, so has the concept of "portfolio career." Others might call it a "slash career," referring to the fact that they're a teacher/blogger/consultant/podcaster/speaker.

So while it might take a few more minutes of explanation to tell your 63-year-old Aunt that worked in Nursing for 42 years what you do (and she still might not get it), and you might not have the instant positioning statement that Gina enjoys, there are several advantages:

1. It keeps the work interesting as there's always a new project to work on

2. It allows you always to be learning and developing a broad spectrum of skills

3. You're not tied to one particular client; if one source of income dries up, you can focus on others

4. You can sample different types of work to see what you like best, then focus on what you like

5. Most importantly, you can have multiple income streams

While some solopreneurs might have just a few items in their portfolio — say, a photographer that also does video editing and teaches a class about using Instagram — for others the list can seem limitless. I'm a good example. When my friend Dan (a job ditcher featured in the case studies) first asked me about the various projects I worked on when I first went out on my own as a "slash employee," I was surprised when I went back and listed out all the sources of income:

- Podcast sponsor income
- Teaching at NYU twice per year
- Teaching two Mediabistro classes four times per year
- Mediabistro consulting clients
- Writing for Salary.com twice per month
- Writing for "The Wall Street Journal of China" twice per month
- Writing for Success magazine several times per year
- Social media consulting
- Social media speaking
- Salary negotiation online courses
- Salary negotiation consulting clients
- Salary negotiation speaking
- Hosting a career conference
- Even Airbnb income

Here's the takeaway: A portfolio career isn't for everyone. One downside is that you run the risk of spreading yourself too thin and never really focusing on a single "craft." However, it can make for a great assortment of potential career moves while you're still in exploration mode.

For example, I was already working on about half that list while I was still working full time. This made it a lot less scary to go out on my own when the time came. I already had a solid base to work from. Then over time, I was able to find my groove with certain tasks and eliminate others.

The other advantage is that a portfolio career can often have a *synergistic* effect. When that happens, you're creating something once, but able to monetize it multiple times across different platforms. For example, a consulting client could lead to a case study, which could then be shared in a speech, a book, a blog post, or a podcast.

Chapter 18: Get online

Whether you're building a business that operates primarily online or not, you're going to want some kind of web presence as your side hustle evolves into your next career.

That's not to say you should invest months working with expensive designers and developers before you know if you have a real business or not, but when someone asks what you do or searches online for your services, you better have a site that illustrates that.

A great resource is our first book in this *Business Reimagined* series, *Website Copywriting: The 7 Essential Pages for Online Business Success*, which gives you everything you need to get a website up and running fast.

The first thing you should do before launching your site is to make sure you have a way to start building a tribe of followers. This generally involves offering free content as a "lead magnet" (at Mirasee we call it a "First Impression Incentive") in exchange for a visitor's email address, and then providing them with additional valuable content or a newsletter over time.

This is an obvious route if your plan involves, say, becoming a publisher of books to help musicians run their bands more efficiently or a personal trainer that helps busy new parents find the time to work out. You're going to want to start building a list of rock stars in the first case and moms in the second, so that by the time your book comes out or you're ready to start teaching, you have a base of customers eagerly awaiting your offer.

But the tactic works well in professions you might not expect as well. For example, my friend Scott runs a financial planning business. Each week, he puts out a newsletter that covers current topics, such as dips in the market, tips for retirement, and even personal news about his latest triathlon adventures. I also have an attorney friend who puts out informative emails and hosts networking events each quarter.

While investments and legal matters might not be the sexiest topics for a newsletter, what this does is keep my friends' businesses top of mind for their clients throughout the year.

You might not need a lawyer now, but if you buy a house in 6 months and need someone to look over a mortgage agreement, simply by virtue of being in your field of awareness on a regular basis, there's a good chance they'll be someone you consider. And while I might already have a financial planner, if a friend asks for a recommendation, Scott is at the top of my list.

Start building your network before you need it. Having a solid website and a growing collection of followers is yet another example of doing things the "right" way as you transition away from the corporate world.

Chapter 19: Go with the flow

OK, so you've been hustling for a few months now, putting in the extra time, building up some clients, and seeing some traction. What next?

Take a step back and look at the flow of your business.

What's working and what's not? Are you spending your time working on the things you thought you would be when you researched the business? Is the amount of revenue coming in likely to increase when you quit your job and you're able to put in more hours?

In our online course training program, *Course Builder's Laboratory*, after hustling and putting out a test pilot course, we recommend one of three options:

1) Scale

The first option is continuing in the same direction and growing your business. If your side hustle experiment is doing well, make any needed adjustments to increase efficiency and allow for growth, and otherwise continue with more of the same.

Congratulations! Your research and hustle has paid off, you've found a good niche, and you're well on your way to escaping the traditional 9-to-5.

2) Iterate

The second option is for situations in which some things are going right, but you're not getting quite the traction you need. It's called iterating, which means tweaking your current business model while staying in the same basic field. So let's say you're trying the portfolio career and are consulting, speaking, and writing about social media.

But throughout the process, the topic that is resonating the most is specifically around Instagram. Of the four consulting clients that you manage to get, 3 of them are local small businesses and they start to have great success.

If that's what's gaining traction, bringing in revenue, and is something you enjoy, then you might iterate on your current strategy by letting your brand evolve from "The social media guy" into "The Instagram consultant for local small businesses."

3) Pivot

The final option occurs when you're not seeing any traction at all in your side hustle. It could be that the path you chose turned out to be completely different than you expected. Or maybe clients just didn't understand your unique selling proposition, so the sales weren't coming. It could be any number of reasons, but even though it may be disappointing, it's not a bad thing.

In fact, this is *exactly* why you tried to launch your business on the side the right way, while you still had a full-time job. If you did things correctly, you didn't rush out and drop $100,000 on a Food Truck in pursuit of being the Taco King of Tuscon.

Instead, you spent a month working on a friend's Food Truck to see if it was for you. Perhaps it left such a (bad) impression, that you vowed never to work in the food industry at all. Go back to your research and pivot. Try something new… you know, like being the Treehouse King of Tulsa.

The takeaway here is that you have to be open to what the market is telling you. While you can't expect success overnight, you do need to examine your options with a clear vision and look for ndicators that your new business idea has legs before making the final leap.

Step 5:
Quitting Day

Chapter 20: Making a graceful exit

Quitting day is finally here!

No matter how things have evolved over the past few months, from your wake-up call to your research and hustle, you probably have a great story to tell. If things have gone according to plan, your side gig is showing great promise, and you're ready to commit to the quit day you marked on your calendar.

While the temptation for a dramatic exit might be huge, there's a right way and a wrong way to handle things.

We established in the introduction that a beer-drinking, profanity-laced, emergency-slide-jumping exit isn't the best way to go. Less obvious is bragging to your boss how amazing your new can't-fail gig is going. Hint: it might not always be going so great.

So while we don't want to suck all the fun out of things, you want people to be saying, "They handled that with class" as opposed to, "The way they handled that was crass."

Here are some tips to keep in mind:

1) Adhere to the chain of command

The most respectful way to leave your job is to tell your boss first, then the people that work for you, then others that need to know, such as other employees, vendors, clients, and so on. While it's tempting to reveal your grand plan to other co-workers before the big day, you need to be able to trust them.

However, good gossip is hard to contain. Upper management hates surprises, and if word leaks and everyone in the company knows you're leaving before your boss does, it can be uncomfortable. Following the chain of command can go a long way to a positive exit.

2) Control your emotions and don't burn bridges

While angrily telling off the boss might make you feel

good in the moment, it's going to reflect badly on your integrity down the line.

You never know how things are going to work out, so be wary of telling your boss "how you really feel" on the way out. You might need a recommendation down the line, and word gets around in a small industry.

The same goes true for any exit interviews with Human Resources. The question, "So why are you leaving?" sounds innocent enough, and you might truly want to help, but choose your words wisely.

Everyone can be gracious when things are going well, but taking the high road when situations change shows your true character should your paths cross again.

3) Evaluate your timeline

In cases with high-level executives or when sensitive company information is at stake, someone from HR – and possibly security – may instantly appear to confiscate your ID and escort you out of the building.

In other situations, you may be asked to stay on staff for a few more days, allowing you to have a "soft exit," wrapping up projects with existing clients and transferring knowledge to whoever will be taking over your job (always an awkward transition).

Determining which scenario is happening to you will dictate how quickly you need to do the rest of your tasks.

4) Back up your files

One thing every company fears most is a disgruntled employee stealing private company information on their way out. To be clear, a scenario where a departing salesperson grabs their "Rolodex" of client names with the intention of luring them to their new business is both illegal and unethical.

I want to emphasize that I am not advocating taking any company property that doesn't belong to you. The fact is, most employment contracts specify that everything you do and create while at the company is legally theirs. No questions asked.

However, what about retrieving personal information from your work computer? It's a good practice to keep your work files and personal files completely separate from each other anyway, but if the only place the seating chart spreadsheet for your upcoming wedding resides is on your company laptop, your boss will understand if you grab that.

In the middle can be a gray area. What if you work at a non-profit and there are photos of you at a charity event that you hosted for the company? What if you work at an advertising agency and edited an award-winning video, and want to use that in your portfolio? The relationship you have with your employer will dictate how these questions are answered.

5) Get everything in writing

In some cases, there might be a lot of details to wrap up as you leave.

Considerations include:

- Determining your last day
- Receipt of your last paycheck
- Claiming unused vacation time
- Bonus eligibility
- Continuation of health benefits
- Retirement savings accounts

It's tough to process everything at once, and they'll probably need to give HR a few days to sort things out, so be sure they give you everything in writing. Do not sign anything until you've had time to go through all the details and ask any questions.

6) Control the message

This is one of the most important steps in the process, but one that few people consider. In the new economy, workers essentially need to be their own publicist.

It's a sad fact that any kind of office turmoil will immediately be followed by office gossip. Human nature dictates that there will be some people thrilled to be the first person to inform everyone, "Did you hear the news? Joe just quit!"

However, like a game of telephone, in some cases, "Joe gave notice" becomes "Joe got fired" or "I heard Joe just told the boss to go screw himself" or "Joe's going to try and start his own business. Good luck with *that*."

You want your business to start off on the right foot, so why not make a concerted effort to control the message?

To your old company and co-workers, say what a privilege it was working with them, help them with the transition as best you can, and offer to keep in touch with them in the future.

Then if you like, talk about your new venture. Say how it's a decision you've been taking seriously for the past few months, and share a few of the steps you took to get to this point. Most people will be impressed, and it might even lead to more clients.

Let me finish up with the best case scenario as I see it.

Back in Chapter 6, I told you the story of my New Year's wake-up call and the eight-month plan to leave the software startup I was working at. After months of planning and execution, quit day finally arrived, and I set up a meeting with my boss

I thought long and hard about what I was going to say, sincerely thanking him for the opportunity he had given me (I was just the third employee). I walked through some of the highlights we had enjoyed over the previous four years, and what we had accomplished together. Then I told him about the new opportunity I had manifested. My boss sat quietly, intently listening while I said my peace.

When I finally finished speaking, he paused and said to me, "Jim, when the first words out of your mouth were 'I'm giving my notice,' I instantly thought about ten different ways to try and convince you to stay.

But after four years, I know you pretty well. I've seen how much fun you have running the office fantasy football league, talking trash with everyone during lunch. I've seen how you simply light up when you're immersed in sports and stats and competition.

So now that I hear what you're going to do… that you're moving to a new city and pursuing your dream job in sports and doing that for a living… I realize there's no way I could possibly talk you out of it. So, best of luck."

And best of luck to you as well. On to the case studies.

Case Studies

Chapter 21: About the Case Studies

Hi, and welcome to the *How to Quit Your Job* Case Studies, where you'll see stories of how people quit their jobs.

While doing research for this book, I reached out to friends, family, and other entrepreneurs, and the response was overwhelming. It's amazing to get responses from so many people that love what they're doing and to see how willing they are to share the story of how they got there. At one point as I neared my deadline, I actually got *too many* good ideas and had to politely decline additional stories.

I posed the question as one of two options:

1) Looking for people who had a plan for quitting their job the "right way" … setting a deadline, putting aside funds, figuring out what they were best at, and transitioning smoothly (ideally unhappy corporate job -> entrepreneurship)

2) The spectacularly "wrong way" … the impulsive, overturning-desks, flipping-off-the-boss, burning-bridges, no-future-in-sight, $9-in-the-bank way

Let me give you a few of the quick hits:

Entrepreneur Peter Shankman wrote, "Woke up one day and said, 'If I fail, I'll get a job.' 18 years later, haven't had to do that."

Brian Clark from Rainmaker Digital and CopyBlogger quickly replied to that comment, "Same for me, thank god."

Gretchen Behnke wrote, "I think I quit the right way. When my first idea of what I would do next didn't turn out to be the thing I wanted to do, I was able to do high-paid consulting at my old company while I figured out the right thing."

My friend Cathy had a unique path, saying, "How about corporate -> actress -> corporate -> entrepreneurship?"

Cory Huff, the author of *How to Sell Your Art* said, "I built a side hustle for four years, and when I quit, I trained my own replacement. Still on great terms with everyone."

Christina Hagopian, who runs her own design firm Hagopian Ink, shared the following, "I was in the process of buying equipment in a fire sale and saving a nest egg to start out on my own when I was laid off. I had about three months before I was going to do it and it just made me start earlier."

My friend James Rose says, "Haha... Definitely #1. Spreadsheets and calculations to work out average spending, initial required wage, how much to put away, and how long it would last if things hit the fan."

Designer Jessica Rea admits, "I'm in the 'spectacularly wrong way' camp... but I made it anyway!"

One theme I saw come up often was hesitation due to fear.

Amanda Cook told me, "I think I did it the right way. The one thing that's different about me is I kept thinking, 'When I have $X in the bank, then I'll quit.' Then I'd get that amount and then say, 'Well, that's not quite enough, when I get X amount THEN I'll really quit!' It went on like that for over a year, until I realized that it wasn't about the specific amount of money, it was the fear! So then I just quit. Best Decision Ever!!!"

As you can see, each person has a unique story. In the upcoming case studies, we'll go a bit deeper.

Note that in some cases, because they share personal and company details, my contacts have asked to stay anonymous, so I've changed their name — but not the story itself.

What you'll find is that each person did things their own way, and that's the takeaway. So be informed, be inspired, and use each story as inspiration for how you want to plan your escape.

Enjoy.

Chapter 22:
Case Study 1 - Naomi

Meet Naomi Less, a multi-skilled facilitator, educator, and musician from New York City, who both performs and creates tailor-made trainings and educational experiences for all ages. Personally, I know her as a rock star, since we were in a band together back in the day. I just sat in the back on drums and tried to keep up with her talent. Here is her story.

Naomi worked full time for seven years as Vice President of Programs at an organization, and as a life-long musician, always had creative endeavors on the side.

But as time wore on, she had difficulty managing a more-than-full-time job with her paid creative pursuits and saw the potential for them to be squashed or eliminated. Additionally, her day job was moving from intimate startup energy to a more corporate style, including her having to navigate an additional layer of upper management with a style that did not match her own.

Coincidentally, at the same time, one of her paid creative pursuits presented an opportunity. The organization needed a project person for a multi-year grant, and she was a perfect fit for the role.

She told me, "the confluence of these factors gave me the courage to pursue a different kind of life/career pursuit."

One day the opportunity she was waiting for presented itself. Another organization needed a project person for a multi-year grant, and she was a perfect fit for the role.

She crafted her exit plan, determining how much time she would need to wrap up her old job in good faith and save up a safety net of rent money in case it took her some time to build up her personal business. Then she picked a target quit date.

She presented her pitch, offering to work 20 hours per week for the new organization while freeing up the rest of her schedule to pursue her other creative career projects.

One thing Naomi didn't need to do was much research, as singing, performing, and leading is something she was born to do. It was just a matter of finding the right role.

Regarding the transition from one role to the next, she told me she was very intentional. "I didn't tell a single work colleague. There were some close colleagues out of my office that I knew I would not be able to work within the same capacity in my new position, so I was able to tell them. But for others, I made sure to maintain a great network of connections."

During the process, she actually hired the person that would, in the end, serve as her replacement, but unbeknownst to the new hire, which was difficult on both sides.

She told me, "When I let the person know I was leaving, she was crushed. But I told her that after training her all summer, I felt confident with her carrying out the role I was leaving and that she could step in and step up."

Confident in knowing she had left her role in good hands, with a grin she walked into the CEO's office with a handful of papers as if it was just another meeting, and announced, "OK, so I'm leaving."

For a split second, she got to see a hint of surprise in their eyes, before they ultimately responded with, "What took you so long?"

Lessons Learned

As you can see, Naomi has one of the hybrid jobs we talked about earlier, which allows her stability in one part of her life while letting her pursue multiple creative projects in another. Planning was a big part of the process, as was having the integrity to leave her past position in good hands, no matter what the outgoing situation.

She admits, "The new situation isn't perfect, but it allows me to control my schedule and work with amazing people. Some people just can't drop everything due to their age, family situation, and benefits, but for me, it really works."

You can learn more about this rock star entrepreneur at naomiless.com.

Chapter 23:
Case Study 2 - Joanna

Meet Joanna Penn, an award-winning, *New York Times* best-selling author, who has sold 450,000 books in 74 countries and five languages. But it wasn't always that way. Here is her story.

Joanna worked as a full-time IT consultant for large corporations for 13 years, but always dreamed of writing her own books. After so long in a job she hated, it was time to make it happen.

She started writing in the early mornings before work and on weekends, learning the craft as well as the business of being a writer. But she knew she had to commit in a bigger way to make real change. Joanna asked her Manager if she could work four days per week instead of five and was accepted. It was a small victory at the time, but it scored her one extra day per week to pursue her passion for writing. She started with a business/self-help book and researched traditional publishers, but the slow pace and negative energy just didn't suit her.

Joanna says, "I self-published my first non-fiction book in 2008 and made a lot of mistakes along the way. I didn't sell any books because no one knew who I was. That experience made me determined to learn about marketing, as well as how to become a better writer."

Intrigued with the rise of digital publishing, print-on-demand, and the use of social media as a marketing platform, she started a blog and podcast called *The Creative Penn*. Joanna immersed herself in everything going on in the industry, and became a trusted source for information, while also interviewing hundreds of other authors along the way.

Embracing her side hustle with enthusiasm, she continued to write and learn about the craft as well as publishing and marketing. However, she made a key pivot when she decided to draw on her past education — as a Theology major from Oxford University — and started writing thriller novels alongside her non-fiction.

She continued to write extensively, expanded her audience, learned how to market effectively, worked hard, and published her first thriller novel — blogging about her journey along the way. One book led to a series, and then things took off.

In September 2011, Joanna left her day job as an IT consultant to be a full-time author-entrepreneur. She now has 20 books – 12 fiction and eight non-fiction. She's also an award-winning creative entrepreneur, professional speaker, blogger, and podcaster.

In March 2014, Joanna officially became a *New York Times* and *USA Today* bestselling author as part of "Deadly Dozen," a box-set with twelve thriller and mystery authors.

In September 2015, Joanna surpassed her income as an IT consultant and hired her husband out of his day job, and now they run *The Creative Penn* together.

Lessons Learned

In this example, Joanna followed the classic "right way" to transition from a day job to a dream career. Not only is she writing full-time, but things have come full circle.

She uses her website TheCreativePenn.com to help other aspiring writers get the skills she wishes she had possessed when first starting out.

It's also important to note that Joanna didn't just quit her job when she decided to write that first book. It took her three-and-a-half years of writing, blogging, podcasting and learning new skills alongside her day job before she was making enough money to quit, and then another few years before she reached the same income she had been earning.

Joanna also uses multiple streams of income and doesn't rely on one book or one sales channel. She mixes writing books, selling courses, using affiliate income, and professional speaking to make up her creative business at *The Creative Penn*.

Chapter 24:
Case Study 3 - Alan

Meet Alan Paluska, the President of a logistics company in Atlanta. Or as my friends and I like to call him, "Alan! Alan! Alan!" (If you missed the inside joke, Google that phrase to see a video with about 10 million views). While his career transition mostly follows the traditional narrative, there are definitely some twists and turns. Here is his story.

I met Alan and his wife several years ago at an annual car event, and we quickly became friends. It's the type of gathering where everyone is on vacation, and the focus is on three things: the people, the cars, and the scenic, twisting roads of the Blue Ridge Mountains. There's not a lot of talk about work, to the point where most people don't even know what the other attendees do in their traditional day job.

However, when I put out the call for stories, Alan was all business. He saw my request, pinged me via instant message, and said, "Call me."

Today was a work day, and Alan was a busy man. Not one to mince words, he jumped right to his wake-up call: "In my last job, I was working for a boss that was eccentric, impulsive, and obsessive." With plenty of connections to go with his experience, he knew it was time to go out on his own.

What makes Alan's story unique is his escape plan. While he didn't have a non-compete clause at his current position, he felt that if his boss found out about the plans for his new business, he'd shut him down and make his life miserable.

So when his quit day came, and it was time to give his notice, he decided to use a little misdirection. When his boss asked what his new venture was about, he said he was going to a *completely* different company in a *completely* different role to throw him off the scent and cause him to let his guard down.

In his previous role, Alan was consulting about the software that large shippers used to coordinate their logistics. He saw an opportunity and market opening where he could use his existing skills in the same field, but instead, helping companies with the trucks themselves.

Alan has hustled, adapted, and grown his new business, Power One Logistics (PowerOneLogistics.com), ever since. But there's one more part of the story to cover.

While we mentioned the misdirection that happened on quitting day, let's talk about discovery day. Alan was able to keep his new venture under wraps for about 6-8 months before his old boss found out and asked him to dinner.

His reaction? The old boss offered to buy him out!

Lessons Learned

As you might guess, Alan turned him down. He told me, "I'm really enjoying all the freedom that comes with running my own business, so the last thing I wanted was to go back to having a boss again."

When I asked him about his thoughts on his misdirection, his philosophy was this: "The whole process is a game of poker… you don't want to tip your hand at any time."

Chapter 25:

Case Study 4 - The Merrymaker Sisters

Meet Carla and Emma Papas, two amazing Australians also known as the Merrymaker Sisters. They both used to work in the Australian Government, and from an outsider's point of view, they probably had "good jobs;" Carla in social media, Emma in internal events. But soon they would launch their own business and never look back. Here is their story.

One doesn't so much *meet* the Merrymaker Sisters as much as you get *pulled into their orbit*. This was the case when I met them for the first time at the 2016 Tropical Think Tank conference. They had attended the year before, and in the first day or so before things kicked off, I had only heard others speak about them as if they were some kind of mysterious, legendary, Tasmanian devils of pure happiness and joy. Turns out that was about right.

With no doubt that they're sisters and rarely leaving each other's side, the energy that emanates from this pair, powered by spirited Australian accents, is nearly as bright as their smiles. If you questioned 1,000 people and asked them to guess if the sisters A) worked for the government or B) were happiness advocates for healthier eating and living a better life, not a single person would choose option A. And yet, that's how their story begins.

While they often complained about their government jobs, their transition to entrepreneurship was more of a slow revelation than a sudden wake-up call. When they first started their Merrymaker Sisters website, it was just a blog, where they shared their thoughts and posted favorite recipes. But one thing was clear. *They loved it.*

They told me, "We loved doing it every single spare second that we had. It started to gain traction, which was totally unexpected and totally amazing that our recipes and advice were helping others."

When they first heard the phrase "follow your bliss," a huge light went off for them. They realized that they were LUCKY enough to have found their bliss… the thing that brought them so much happiness and joy… the thing that when they did it, time just ceased to exist. "We could work on the site for hours, but it wasn't work, it was just fun… pure bliss."

They continued to work their corporate government jobs (now complaining daily) while side hustling on the blog. Then they heard another key phrase: "What you focus on grows." That was the aha! moment that really took them over the edge.

They thought… "What if we STOPPED complaining about the jobs we hated, the work we dreaded every day, and moved our focus to all the GOOD in our lives? What if we had all of our hours to focus on Merrymakers? Surely it would grow. Surely we could turn it into a profitable business."

With this inspiration and a positive mindset at the start of 2014, they crafted their plan and set a goal to quit their jobs by the end of the year. The strategy was to save money and create income streams for the blog since they were making minimal money at the time.

The way they executed that strategy, however, might seem a bit risky to some. Rather than put any money aside into savings, they reinvested anything and everything they had back into the blog and their business. While this might not be the best route for an older entrepreneur with a family to support and a mortgage to pay, for two twenty-something sisters with an "all or nothing" attitude, it made total sense. While there wasn't much revenue, they were building something more critical: a large and passionate community of fans.

They told me, "We look back now and realize that what helped us was being naive. We always had such a passion and are always so proud of the work we do, even if we cringe at the stuff we did back then. But that positive mindset helped us take action and be fearless in our creations."

Their research phase was in the form of reading blogs about blogging, getting inspired by other online businesses, and focusing on all the good things that were going on in their lives. They had in their minds the quote from the documentary *Finding Joe*, "When you follow your bliss, doors will open where there were once only walls." This started coming true… the more they focused on Merrymakers, the more opportunities came their way.

The sisters didn't have to overanalyze their new career direction before leaving since they were already doing it and were getting plenty of positive feedback from their following. They just knew this was their mission. But they did have to pay attention to the bottom line and run the numbers.

Carla told me, "One day at our government jobs we had had enough. Emma did some calculations by herself based on the bills we had to pay and how much money we needed to JUST survive. She broke down the numbers into goals, what we needed to achieve each month, and how to do that. It seemed doable, even though we had never done it before! So we thought, 'Well… yeah! We can do that!' We also had the thought in the back of our mind that if we DID quit our jobs, that we'd just HAVE to make it happen… because there's no other way. There wasn't a safety net of good government pay every fortnight!"

Their initial plan to ditch their day job was to ask for one year of leave without pay, figuring it would keep their parents happy. That didn't work out so well.

Their bosses offered them the option of going part time or taking a few days off here and there. Emma said, "We walked out of the office feeling depressed, and angry at the managers."

So five minutes passed, and they hatched up a new plan:

First, they would quit.
Second, they would lie to their parents about what happened.

The first part worked like clockwork. They realized that even if they had the year without pay, that it was NEVER their intention to go back to their soul-sucking office jobs. Why would they even want that option? It was a toxic workplace filled with people who hated their jobs (and their lives!).

Emma explains, "So we drafted identical resignation emails to our managers. Same title. Same message." (If you've met the sisters, this won't surprise you). "We read each other's emails, checked for any spelling errors, and said... 3.... 2.... 1... SEND! At exactly the same time, with the same email, we resigned. And then... we went to lunch! We literally *skipped* out of the office. It was amazing."

Carla continued, "We only worked a short drive from our house, so we went home, made a healthy smoothie and cheered ourselves on as we realized we were about to follow our dreams. We had a deck of "oracle cards" which we'd just been getting into, which basically provide inspiring messages for moments when you need a 'sign' of some sort. We shuffled the cards and picked one at random for the moment."

The random card that came up that day? It said, "Time to go."

Next up was dealing with their family.

"We decided that we'd keep the news from our parents, and tell them that our company accepted our leave without pay. This would keep Mum and Dad happy, so they wouldn't stress about us."

And yet, there was something they couldn't resist. "We immediately blasted out the good news on Facebook."

Like so many others have learned the hard way, the internet and secrets do not go well together.

"What we failed to remember was that our Mum and Dad had friends on Facebook, whom we were also friends with. Eventually, they found out, and we had to come clean. At first, they were so worried. We'd given up stable jobs, complete with health coverage and superannuation" (that's Australian for retirement savings).

But just one month into Merrymaking full time, their parents realized how much happiness it brought their daughters. They were suddenly two very different girls. "They were happy because we were happy!"

It also took some time for others to fully grasp their new venture. "All of our friends and work colleagues couldn't believe it. They were shocked and at the same time, probably a little jealous."

Lessons Learned

I asked the sisters to sum up their story. "We always say that since we quit our government jobs, we haven't worked a day in our lives. Merrymaking isn't work for us. It's passion. It's fun. It's pure bliss. We have loved every minute of our lives, which is just AMAZING."

Of course, just because it's fun, doesn't mean it's not without challenges. "It's hard. Definitely. It's hard. We question ourselves; we have moments of doubt. But we come back to our one big lesson that everything is either a blessing or a lesson."

"Our journey is there for us to take. If we take one way, and it doesn't work out, then we just change it up and take another road. We've learned to trust ourselves. To listen to our intuition and to just ENJOY every single second of life. What is life but one big adventure?"

"We always think back to the moment when we quit our jobs, and we realize that the bigger risk was STAYING in those corporate jobs and looking back when we're 50 years old with regret and wondering 'What if?'"

Instead, they decided to act now and say, "What if we followed our bliss? What if we gave it a shot? We realized the bigger risk was NOT going after our dream."

Learn more about the Merrymaker Sisters at http://www.themerrymakersisters.com/

Chapter 26:
Case Study 5 - Dan

Meet Dan. He was a teacher for many years, working his way from a substitute, to a Teaching Assistant, to teaching a college-level course. He was never completely sure that teaching was what he wanted to do with the rest of his life, but it was good for the time being, and there were aspects of the job that he liked. Then one day, all that changed. Here is his story.

I met Dan (not his real name) a few years back when he was a student in one of my Professional Studies classes at New York University. Like the city itself, these courses drew a diverse set of students, from business professionals looking to learn new skills, to international visitors still grasping the language. After the first round of homework, Dan's writing stood far above the others, so it wasn't a shock to find out that he was an English teacher. Here is more about his background:

"I was a teacher for many years, but it wasn't a consistent position. I performed lots of jobs within the schools I worked in, working my way from a sub to a TA to a teacher of college-level courses. There were certainly aspects of the job that I liked: the students (well, most of the students), the extracurricular activities that I ran, and my colleagues (well, most of my colleagues). There were also times that were difficult, but I fought through them."

"Then one day, that all changed. I can't explain exactly what the catalyst was — maybe a combination of things — but I suddenly woke up and realized that I wasn't enjoying my job. It's unpopular to want to end a career because you 'don't like it.' I had worked all these years to get to this point, and I was making a good salary, so why quit? Besides, I had all the perks of being a teacher: a pension, summers off, and shortened work days. (Ok, that last one is a lie… my typical work day was 10 hours long). Oh, and to top it off, I also had a newborn!"

The incongruity of how he *thought* he should feel and how he was *actually* feeling surfaced in an ironic way.

"I was working with one of my senior classes, and the topic was 'dream job.' Here I was trying to teach these students to pursue the best career for themselves, and yet I was being a hypocrite. I suddenly realized, *this ain't it for me.* That feeling got worse as the pressures of the job increased throughout the school year. The stress didn't seem worth it anymore, and I didn't see myself doing this for the next 30 years. I knew in my heart that I would change careers eventually. Why not now?"

When we talked about choosing your quit date in Chapter 6, one of the options was timing things around any kind of natural break or downtime in your industry. Few other jobs lend themselves to that as much as teaching.

"I look at a school year as one complete entity. Leaving in the middle is certainly *not* recommended, and regardless of how I felt toward the profession, I still had a duty to my students. Leaving wouldn't happen until the year ended. I knew somewhere around the middle of February that I would be looking elsewhere, but I had no idea how."

Despite his plan, Dan's Quit Day did not turn out as expected.

"Funny story about giving my notice - I didn't. They gave me *their* notice. They beat me to the punch, which, honestly, was a little deflating. That was going to be my shining moment when I took control of my life. My quitting story. The one I could tell at lunch to inspire people. When I jumped on the desk, stomped my feet, and got to scream 'No, *you're* out of order!'. And walk out with my head held high.

But none of that happened. It was much lamer. The monologues that I perform in my head rarely happen in real life. It was quick. I was called in at the end of the day and let go. I wouldn't be returning for the next school year. It was over within 5 minutes.

The reaction was interesting. Since there were still two months left in the school year, I controlled the message, only telling my closest friends at work first, then branching it out. They went to bat for me, even going as far as calling a meeting and expressing their discontent to the boss. I didn't ask them to, because as I explained to them, I was at peace. The stress was gone. I was going to leave anyway."

While many professionals can seamlessly pivot from one skill set to the next as they transition, Dan found himself with two issues. The first was that he didn't know what he wanted to do, and the second was that he'd need to completely revamp his value proposition to future employers.

"My resume was very education-centered and hadn't been updated in about six years. My LinkedIn page was crap. The first part of my plan involved updating those important documents and talking to people about it. I met with and called some trusted mentors to get their take, as well as my family. I got my family on board, and they're behind me 100%. I'm not the first teacher to leave the profession, and I won't be the last. My newborn even came to me in a dream and told me, in perfect Queen's English, that I have his support. That last part I made up."

While his quit day was less than satisfying, he had the support of his family, was free to explore any option, and was ready to take action. Here's how he's approached the research phase:

1. I used the last month to totally rewrite my resume from scratch and get my LinkedIn profile to a respectable place.

2. I started logically working through the goals of what I wanted my next gig to look like. I'm searching for something that will make me happy and get me excited, and not suck my soul: a job with creativity, flexibility, and passion. As my wife says, "That's what everybody wants!" I agree, but I just don't know why everybody isn't going for it.

3. I've been reading up on the whole "gig based" idea of work and how it's the newest trend and may become more of a permanent and mainstream way of working in the future. The idea of multiple income streams has always fascinated me since putting all your eggs in one basket seems really dumb, but it's what most people do.

4. To help me get to the place where I want to be, I've started speaking to people and setting up meetings. I'm not even close to the number of networking events or connections that I need. It would probably be easier if I knew what I wanted to do… then I could target the people in that field that I really need to speak to. There is a whole lot of soul-searching going on right now. And a lot of drinking.

Lessons Learned

I included Dan's story because I wanted to show that quitting your job isn't always about inspirational quotes from a book, *skipping* out of the office on your quit day, and having everything filled with sunshine (damn you, Merrymaker Sisters).

Rather, it's about the *process*. For some, it might take months, and for others, it might take years to fully embrace your craft. But as long as you're on the right path, you will succeed in the end.

As Dan's soul-searching continues, he's found himself tapping into what he's truly passionate about, allowing himself to think about jobs he might not have considered before.

"I'm attempting to make at least one positive move every day. I've been looking into taking another Professional Studies class, but this time at FIT (Fashion Institute of Technology). I like clothes, and most men can't dress themselves. There might be something there. Aside from that, I'm hoping that there's a way I can use the skills that I acquired from my job as a teacher and combine them with the skills and experience that I have from the various projects and other jobs that I've had outside of a school setting to find that thing that works. I would be content with one full-time job, or several part time jobs. As long as I hit the number that I need to hit, I'm a happy guy."

To be continued…

Chapter 27:
Case Study 6 - Nick

Meet Nick. He used to work in corporate finance for a Fortune 500 company in Miami, putting in 60-80 hour weeks before realizing he was just working to pay his bills and he wasn't getting ahead. He decided to move to New York, start his own business, and in the first year doubled his income and traveled to 14 countries. Here is his story.

I met Nick (not his real name) at a conference in New York, where he was a volunteer. It was clear from the start that he was already very smart and yet continually thirsting for knowledge, pulling any information he could from the speakers, attendees, and those around him. We talked careers, salary negotiation, and the future of work.

At the time, he worked in corporate finance in Miami for a Fortune 500 company, but he knew he wanted a change. His wake-up moment was when he realized he was working just to pay the bills. He wasn't getting ahead in his career, he didn't love his job, and he even had a side gig to supplement his income.

While there were many perks about working in Florida, such as the weather, the cost of living, and no state income tax, he wanted to be where the action was. Like many young professionals, he weighed the pros and cons of New York City vs. Silicon Valley.

From there, he did things the "right way," by using his vacation time and weekends from his job to explore both cities to make sure he was making an informed decision. He volunteered for events, went to Meetup groups, and lined up some interviews, all while crashing with friends to keep costs low. While all of us have heard so much about the startup culture, he wanted to experience it personally, so he went to conferences such as TechCrunch Disrupt in San Francisco, Collision in New Orleans, and 99U in NYC.

When the opportunity to join an exclusive incubator training program in San Francisco appeared, it was very tempting. While talking over coffee, I was pretty sure that he'd jump at the chance. The tuition for the program was pretty steep, but it all but guaranteed a decent-paying job at a startup once the program concluded. However, Nick showed restraint, analyzed every angle (including the cost of the program and cost of living), and took a long-term view.

Knowing that he could always join the program the following spring, he committed to staying in Florida for several more months. He even took an additional part-time job in order to go into "extreme money saving mode" in the short term and be better positioned financially in the long term.

When the time was right, he took action:

"One weekend I just quit. I had had enough, and that was that. My boss was cool. His boss was not. Most people were sad to see me leave. There wasn't much drama, except for the relief for me that I could finally breathe."

Lessons Learned

In the end, Nick decided to move to New York to experience the city where dreams are made of, and to take a risk on a career as an independent consultant.

His advice? You can't just guess at what you *think* you want to do, you need to hustle, do the research first, and then experience it.

"For me, the key was hard work and research, research, research. In addition to my full-time job, I took jobs waiting tables, helping friends with Excel, tutoring students, and doing consulting - anything to make sure I had the cash cushion I needed and was learning something new. I read countless books, took dozens of meetings, went on interviews, and just took everything in as I went, investing in my own personal knowledge base. Today I am still studying my butt off to get more skilled and better at everything I can."

So how did things turn out?

"When I look back, the best thing I have ever done in my life was to move to New York City (I Live in Brooklyn today). I knew that the opportunity to go back to corporate would always exist, so why not take the risk? In the year that I've been in NY, I have made more than double what I made yearly at the previous job. Not only that, but I have traveled to 14 countries in the past 12 months, have my own personal assistant, and have also learned additional skills I wanted to pick up."

Chapter 28:
Case Study 7 - Andy

Meet Andy. After a wake-up call incident with his current company, he went out on his own and had his best year ever in terms of income. His take on Quit Day? Maybe it's ok to take a stand for truth, even if it means burning bridges. Here is his story.

I met Andy (not his real name) the same way many people meet each other in the traditional working world — we were both confined to cubicles just six feet from each other. We reconnected later on when I was working for myself and he was working at one company while freelancing for another.

"I was looking to get out of my primary full-time job for a few reasons. The biggest was that the company wasn't making any money, and I knew how much funding they had raised. The other, but just as important reason, was that one guy, in particular, the owner and founder — let's call him Rick — was brash, arrogant, and very much I KNOW EVERYTHING."

Meanwhile, "The husband and wife team that ran the agency I was freelancing for was great, but it was very new. I was able to give them a few hours on two clients, a big but boring brand, and a super new, but super cool brand."

"When I first started working with them, what I had to offer was pretty vague. But after three months, I saw a huge opening in tying together all their media channels into a whole narrative arc, as my ultimate value add."

"Suddenly I had more business than I could handle, and I knew the time to cut the cord at my primary job had come."

While the influx of new work gave him the confidence to move on, one event, in particular, was his wake-up call moment.

"I was in a meeting pitching myself and my freelance client to a very big, very well-known fashion brand, and

I knew I had done some work for them at my full-time job."

"What I didn't know, was that Rick, the brash, I-Know-Everything owner, had broken the terms of the deal. He never paid for the rights to music that was used in a video, which I then promoted to more than a million people. Essentially, he let me walk directly into a trap."

Andy smoothed things over as best he could, but it was clear that he was a net detriment to that endeavor.

When he got back to the office, he told each of the three other owners of the company what had happened and that as a result, he was cutting ties.

Here is where Andy decided to ignore the advice of not burning bridges.

"As I gave my notice, my last line was this: Rick is a reputational hazard. His poor decisions and flat out bad manners have cost this company money; it has cost me money personally, and I'm willing to bet it has affected each of your business concerns as well. Sorry, it's the truth. Goodbye."

As I stood there with my mouth on the floor, Andy added, "And yes, Rick was sitting right in front of me when I said that."

Lessons Learned

"While we didn't close the deal with the well-known fashion brand that day, my client was very understanding. I'm still working with them and now have seven clients, plus three additional ones on my own."

"My firm is doing well, really well. In fact, my rate is now $250/hour, and this will be my best year ever in terms of income. I have a 2-year-old son, and the job allows me to spend more time with him, set my own hours, and work with only the clients that I want. My goal is to present a talk at SXSW in 2018."

Yes, but what about the way Andy quit? I asked him if he would give that same advice to someone else… if there were a situation where it's ok to burn bridges. He responded:

"Can I be honest with you? It was the best feeling in the world. One of the owners came back to me afterward and gave me one of those outside clients. So maybe the moral is: it's not burning bridges if it's true. When you have your facts straight, and something really wrong has happened, then maybe making a bit of a scene is OK."

Chapter 29:
Case Study 8 - Kevin

Meet Kevin Basham. He was a national sales manager for a UK-based environmental services business – a good job with a good salary and perks. But his reality was a lot different. He quit without having a plan, but overcame several challenges to launch his own business from nothing and grow it to seven figures. Now, he's determined to do things the right way and is strategically planning his future career in helping others. Here is his story.

I met Kevin at a conference called Tropical Think Tank, and he was a little bit different. It wasn't just his British accent (there were others with those), or his intense desire to learn (everyone fell into that group). What made him different was that at an entrepreneurship conference where everyone had some kind of personal brand, multi-platform message, or digital product they were trying to scale (guilty on all three counts), he was involved in something far less sexy: recycling plastic.

While I'd find out later how impressive his entrepreneurial skills were at his current business, here's what impressed me most: he was at the conference to strategize his long-term plan as an entrepreneur. Really long-term. So while this book aims to help those that want to escape the working world in 6-12 months, I think it's equally as helpful to see someone with a much longer exit plan.

Let's allow Kevin to start at the beginning.

"I was a national sales manager for an environmental services business. I had a nice car, good salary, and generally good perks to the job. To the outside world, it looked like I had a great life. However, the reality was very different."

"I felt unappreciated, and because the company was struggling, they relied on me to pull in lots of new business. During my first 10 months, I pulled in over £1million of new sales. However, their biggest client went into administration." (In the UK, akin to bankruptcy).

"The culture in the business wasn't particularly great. I couldn't be myself and never felt like I could fit in. One of the directors humiliated me a number of times during team meetings, and colleagues made personal remarks about me."

I asked him if he had a plan. Did he set a time frame? Put aside savings?

"No, I just quit. I hated it so much that I didn't care about the money anymore. I was very unhappy. To make matters worse, at the time I also had a huge amount of personal debt, but I managed to survive and get through that."

What did that feel like?

"When I gave my notice, I felt upset and relieved at the same time. I was upset because of the pain it had caused me, and how I think things should have worked out differently. One of the directors didn't speak to me for the whole of my notice period. He clearly had issues of his own, and looking back, it probably wasn't to do with me. But at the same time, I was relieved to be out of that situation."

Now without a job, I asked Kevin how he decided what he wanted to do next.

"Through my network, I landed a couple of consulting gigs to keep the money coming in. I provided an outsourced business development service and ended up landing three clients over a few months. I then joined forces with a business partner and we ended up starting a recycling business."

Kevin says he wishes he could have tested these new businesses before making the leap and quitting his job.

"I really should have, but I was stuck and didn't know what to do, or how it all would work. In hindsight, I should have had some clients to work for before I left, but things were so crappy that I just wanted out. When there's no other option than to try and make money without a traditional job, you'll find a way to succeed. It's the most uncertain and stressful method. However, it worked out for me."

Fortunately, Kevin was able to evaluate his businesses on the fly, go with the flow, and pivot accordingly.

"I knew the business development and marketing consultancy wouldn't work long term. Our clients were hugely demanding and we often over-promised. Setting up the recycling company was a big adjustment, but we saw a business that could be scaled and potentially sold one day."

Lessons Learned

In Kevin's case, the story thus far has a happy ending, and he's laying the foundation for an even more fulfilling lifestyle down the line.

His first transition was from a terrible corporate job to traditional entrepreneurship — running a company.

"I'm still running the plastics recycling business, and we've grown it from zero to a solid 7-figure business in 5 years. We had no investment, little knowledge, and I was carrying personal debt. Now my debts are gone, I've worked my tail off for years, and I'm in a much more secure place."

"When your back is up against the wall, you do anything you can. I think having no money and no savings to fall back on, drove me so hard to make a successful company. Doing it the other way would have been far less stressful, but the urgency created a massive drive inside me."

With the struggles he went through fresh in his mind, Kevin is looking forward to his second career transition, from a profitable business to solopreneurship — and helping others that are in the situation he was in.

"Looking back, I wish I had more help. Mentors, coaches, and other businesspeople could have helped me, but I didn't know where to start. While I can't put an exact time on when I'll be ready to sell my business, that's not going to stop me from attending conferences, making connections, and planting the seeds right now. I've already developed a website, created a mailing list, started a blog, have an internship program, and coach others. I also plan on starting a podcast. I can't wait for the next step in this journey."

Read Kevin's full story here: www.kevinbasham.com

Chapter 30:
Case Study 9 - Nathan

Meet Nathan (not his real name). He worked at a major cosmetics company, and loved it at first. It was a good company, he enjoyed going to work, and he was self-motivated, staying late and making sure he hit his deadlines. He worked on a team that was very popular with the rest of the company. But then came the inevitable corporate shuffle, and everything went south. He spent several more years there before overcoming his fear and launching his own company, and now he's living in Brazil and launching a new venture. Here is his story.

I'm going to ruin the ending and tell you that everything works out for our friend Nathan. What his story illustrates, however, is how incredibly difficult it can be to make a change. Week after week, month after month, your life rolls on, like some kind of career Terminator. Fear can be a powerful thing, and it often takes significant effort to overcome it. But if you ask anyone about a major life change, most will tell you that most of the fear was unfounded.

Tell us your story Nathan:

"I was working at a major cosmetics company, and for the first three years, it was awesome. I was happy, motivated, working hard, and staying late to make sure I was hitting all my goals. I was the head of the Flash interactive development group, which was kind of a "special operations" team. We developed web apps, slideshows and interactive videos that were not possible with HTML at the time, and all the brands loved us because we were able to create anything they could think of. I felt like I was the star at every company event. Life was good."

Then what happened?

"However, in my fourth year, there was a major disruption. The company transitioned away from Flash, I changed my team, and my group got absorbed into the larger IT department. From here it became hell since we became part of the bureaucracy of a major corporation. Our e-commerce websites were doing great, and corporate profits followed, but the startup feel of my job had ended."

"Moving forward, I was basically doing the minimum to survive at the company. Naturally, management wasn't happy with my workload, so they asked me to take on more work. I indirectly said 'No' because I was scared to decline them outright and leave. Believe it or not, this actually went on for another THREE YEARS. It finally got to the point where they asked me to either step up and do the work or leave. I chose to leave and got three months severance."

How did you handle the transition?

"I had been at the company for seven years, and sadly, I had been mentally preparing to leave for the last four. I started saving considerably, putting almost all of my salary (minus rent) on the side. I stopped going to expensive restaurants, going out, and buying clothes. My initial plan was to look for a job at a startup, but from my research, it looked like the salaries at startups were going to be much lower than my current salary, which was more than six figures, plus stock options."

What did you do next?

"After looking at the startup scene, I got more courage and started to think that I had enough experience and connections to start my own digital agency. I hired a coach to help make the transition from a techie and leading developers, to thinking more about the "business of making software." His rate was $1,000 for three months, 1 hour a week, but it was worth the investment. The coach helped me tremendously on both the professional and personal end. For example, my wife was very scared of the idea of me going out on my own, and the coach helped me with that."

How did you finally decide to jump ship?

"I was out almost every night networking and growing my network on the side. I went to talks, seminars, anything you can think of. If there was a tech / networking / conference / pitch event in NYC, I was there. One of the best ones was one of the last events before leaving work, which was your (Jim's) Reboot Conference about how to leave your day job. I remember I was so inspired by the speakers. At the end of the conference, in order to make sure we acted on what we wanted to do, we wrote a postcard to ourselves and we had to give it to one of the conference organizers so that they could check on us in the future. I remember exactly what I wrote on that card: In two months I am going to leave my job."

Did you "try out" your new career before leaving?

"I did! Almost every day during the week, I would go to networking events after work. I created a name for my company, registered it as an LLC, and was out there selling. I got my first project from someone I met at Digital Dumbo, then another and then another. I closed on three deals in total while I was still at my day job. It was tough, and at times I couldn't keep up. This caused both my full-time job and side hustle job to really suffer."

When did you know it was going to work? Was there a turning point?

"Working with a consultant was great because he gave me confidence and showed me a process and said, 'If you follow this process things will come together.' One of the tasks I had to do to grow my business was to talk to 30 people a day. That was my fuel to get new projects, and getting projects meant hiring freelance developers and designers and growing the business. I was doing marketing, selling, business development, and project management.

Tell me about Quitting Day.

"It all happened behind closed doors. The company wanted things to go quietly. About 2-3 days before my last day, I sent out an email to all my colleagues and everyone was shocked to hear the news. My superior knew that I didn't like my role in the company, but when my colleagues heard the news, people started coming to my desk asking what happened. It was a shock to them. I told them that since my group was absorbed in the IT dept, I wasn't happy anymore, and it is not working out. I couldn't tell them the whole story. It was quite a send-off though. We had about 70 people come out for goodbye drinks. I loved the people I worked with, but I didn't love the big company bureaucracy."

"Once I was out, though, I hit the ground running. That final party was on a Friday, and on Monday I had already rented a shared desk and started contacting people in my network. It took awhile to fully get off the ground. I did a month of consulting, which was horrible, so I decided to put that on hold and focus on growing the business. Nine months from the day I left my corporate job, I won my first major project to do two mobile apps."

"From there, I applied the formula of trying to speak to 30 people a day. Incidentally, it's more of a mindset trick, and I have never hit that number, although my record might be more than 20. I was loving the freedom I had in speaking to my clients and have total control in how I want each project to be executed."

Lessons Learned

How did everything work out?

"Well, I'm still alive after leaving! I was soooo scared of not having a 9-to-5 job that it completely paralyzed me. I think this comes from the way I was brought up. My parents always told me, 'Study hard, finish college, and find a good job at a good company.' So the thought of *not* doing that and try to do something else was terrifying."

"But I want to tell people, don't be afraid, things will always work out. After leaving the company, I had all of these irrational fears, which I now realize are totally normal. Seriously, I started thinking that I was going to end up homeless in Times Square and that my wife and kids would leave me!"

"I've worked with big companies and small startups. I brought in an associate to help me and worked with many vendors. I even got projects from my former employer. I have become a totally different person, thinking more about opportunities and building relationships vs. being a developer and thinking how I am going to keep up learning the programming code syntax to stay current."

"The freedom I had has also allowed me to take on things I never would have imagined. For example, my wife found a job in Brazil that paid 30% more than her current salary, with a lot of benefits, such as paying for school for our twins. We decided to take a chance, and now I am totally dialed into the tech scene in Brazil. I'm even launching a new online subscription business to sell diapers."

"Looking back, making the leap was scary as hell, but I am so happy, and I thank God that I did it. I feel much more relaxed now, and it's less about the money. I exercise, I read spiritual books, and I try to help and be of service to others. I feel like I spent all my life trying to avoid a crisis and be on the safe side, but it was only when I had a crisis that I felt alive, and that propelled me closer towards my dreams in doing something that I love."

"It really was all about overcoming the fear. I was scared. I was scared that my wife would think that it is not fair that I get to quit my job to pursue my dream while she has to work and support us both. I was scared that my family would not understand and think that I am not good. I was scared of making mistakes. Now I realize it paralyzed me from living life to its fullest. The rest is history."

Chapter 31:
Case Study 10 - Phil

Meet Phil Berberian. I met Phil in 2002 while working at ESPN because we had something in common. Ironically, in a company filled to the brim with rabid sports fans who had made it their life goal to work in that industry, we didn't bond over Tom Brady, Tiger Woods, or Trey Wingo. In fact, Phil was an anomaly... barely a sports fan at all. Music was his thing.

The simple reason we connected was that every night at 7, 8, or even 9 pm, long after others had gone home, we were both still in the office, working away. For me, I loved my job and was finishing up work. For him, he had finished up his day-job obligations (he was a contractor) and was working on his side business as an artist manager, songwriter, and music producer. Here is his story.

"Throughout my contract, the company kept trying to bring me on full-time, but I kept resisting." This was a job that had resumes piled up a foot high, yet he enjoyed his setup as contractor by day, music business entrepreneur by night. He had a hybrid job before it was fashionable to do so. Finally, he relented and became a full-time employee, and as luck would have it, we were seated next to each other for the next three years before life took him in a new direction.

"I'm not sure my story is really noteworthy in any way. Much like you, Jim, I don't do anything without a plan. At least nothing major. I like to consider myself spontaneous and a risk taker, sometimes even impulsive, but not when it comes to major life decisions. Those are well thought out. Calculated risks."

But while he had a plan for leaving the corporate world after a reorganization, he had to put his plans on hold just two months later.

"My exit from the corporate world was a combination of two things: 1) Wanting the revenue from my music industry activities to increase in relation to my ESPN revenue, and 2) The reorganization that the company went through meant that I would have to report to Frank @#!%Bucket Baker, which consequently meant that I would have less latitude where my non-ESPN activities were concerned." (I took the liberty of changing Frank's name).

What did your plan look like?

"I made sure that I had enough money saved up to get through six months of abject unemployment in Manhattan. If my recollection serves me right, I tendered my resignation in March 2005. I didn't need to explore new career opportunities or hire a coach or anything since the point of leaving this job was to simply allow me to dedicate more time to focus on my music related activities. But in reality, I just wanted to leave."

What I remember most about Phil's resignation is that none of the employees knew how to handle it. They were extremely confused. First of all, the company was pretty great overall, with decent pay, good benefits, and the chance for amazing perks, like trips to the Super Bowl and "working" at events with high-profile athletes. This was a job that didn't have a lot of turnover.

Second, when people *did* decide to leave, that meant it was for a pretty amazing reason, such as being lured away to a competitor with a huge bump in title and salary.

Therefore, as I sat next to him on his quit day, I heard a lot of conversations like this:

"Hey, Phil! Just wanted to swing by, as I heard that you're leaving. We're going to miss you, man."

"Thanks, Jack."

"So what company are you going to? Is it CBS? Fox? No, wait. I bet it's Yahoo!"

"I'm not sure."

"Err, what do you mean you're not sure? What's your new gig?"

"I don't have another job. I'm just leaving."

"What? What do you mean? You're quitting without another job?"

"Yup."

"What are you going to do?"

"I'm not sure. Work on my music stuff a bit."

While I knew that he wanted to work on his music business more, I remember having a strange feeling, one that I couldn't explain. There seemed to be something more here, and I think he felt it too. His story continues:

"About two months after I left, in May 2005, I found out that my mom was diagnosed with advanced stage cancer. She meant the world to me, and the news was devastating. I dropped everything I was doing to be by her side and stayed with her for months. She passed in December of that year."

Lessons Learned

If you hate your job, are overwhelmed with opportunities, or have no idea what you want to do, it's easy to focus on everything that his happening RIGHT NOW. But sometimes it's only when taking an extremely long-term view, dividing your life into segments, that you can look back and be proud of your path.

After his mom's death, Phil took an extended break and traveled around the world, visiting Armenia, Egypt, Hong Kong, Singapore, Cambodia, Thailand, and Malaysia. When he came back to New York, he had a new plan in mind.

"That's when I made the decision to leave New York City and move to Miami to be with my Dad and siblings and to help him with the family music business, which he'd been discussing with me for years. I was never really interested, but my mom's death was the catalyst that made it happen. The last 10 years have shown me that family is far more important than work."

That being said, Phil can feel the pull of a new chapter in his life. Now married and recently becoming a father himself, the wheels are turning for his next move.

Conclusion

Congratulations! You're ready to quit your job.

For some people — sadly, for many, many people — work is just a means to an end. Some are collecting a decent paycheck and benefits, but those items force them to remain mired in an unfulfilling job that they hate.

Others are both underpaid *and* unhappy at work, trudging through life in slow motion, not unlike the commute they suffer through daily.

But for some, there comes a wake-up call. A moment in life when they realize they want to look back at their life and know that they did something that mattered... a job that made them happy... a craft that played to their strengths... a life that truly meant something besides just paying the rent.

So if you've had your wake-up call, get out there and craft your exit plan, do the fun research, work that side hustle, and mark your quit day.

You'll thank me later.

Quit Your Job Extras

Free PDF Downloads +
Online Video Companion Course

When it comes to making the leap, we want to give you all the tools necessary to quit your job the right way. Get free bonus resources and a discounted price to our online video companion course.

Free PDF Downloads
- Danny Iny's bestselling book, *Engagement From Scratch!*
- Full color Ikigai and Zen Diagram charts
- All 10 case studies in PDF form
- Financial inventory template

Online Video Companion Course – 50% off coupon
Are you a visual learner? You'll love our video-based companion course.

- 60+ minutes of video instructions
- Entertaining and educational storytelling
- Video walk-throughs of the 5-step plan

Get your free PDF downloads and course coupon:

http://mrse.co/quit-your-job-extras

About Danny Iny

Danny Iny (@DannyIny) is the founder of Mirasee, host of the Business Reimagined podcast, best-selling author of multiple books including *Engagement from Scratch!*, *The Audience Revolution*, and *Teach and Grow Rich*, and creator of the acclaimed *Audience Business Masterclass* and *Course Builder's Laboratory* training programs, which have together graduated over 4,000 value-driven online entrepreneurs. He lives in Montreal, Canada with his wonderful wife (and business partner) Bhoomi, and their beautiful baby daughter.

Also by Danny Iny:

- *Teach and Grow Rich: The Emerging Opportunity for Global Impact, Freedom, and Wealth*

- The Audience Revolution: The Smarter Way to Build a Business, Make a Difference, and Change the World

- Engagement from Scratch!: How Super-Community Builders Create a Loyal Audience and How You Can Do the Same!

About Jim Hopkinson

Jim Hopkinson (@HopkinsonReport) is a digital media professional helping to reimagine education and training for the new economy. As Director of Courses at Mirasee, he helps entrepreneurs get the training they need to put their ideas into the world by building and scaling a profitable online business. He is also the author of *Salary Tutor*, and helps ambitious professionals negotiate higher salaries. He lives in New York City, is an avid sports fan and tech geek, and enjoys mentoring young business professionals.

Also by Jim Hopkinson:

- Salary Tutor: Learn the Salary Negotiation Secrets No One Ever Taught You

Also in the *Business Reimagined* series

Website Copywriting: The 7 Essential Pages for Online Business Success

Write your web copy quickly, confidently, and effectively!

If you're trying to figure out how to get impressive results from your website copywriting, everything you need to know is right here in this book.

Today, anyone with a domain name and a design can start a website. But to make your site an effective business tool, you need to create a specific impression and have a message that resonates in order to convert them into loyal followers and customers. This is especially true if you're a "solopreneur" – an individual with a unique skill or message to share and who wants to make the world a better place.

So whether you're a coach or a consultant, an author or a speaker, a math tutor or a magician, this book will teach you the vital copywriting skills required for online business success.

Blog Post Ideas: 21 Proven Ways to Create Compelling Content and Kiss Writer's Block Goodbye

Never run out of blog post ideas again!

A blogger's job is never done. To be successful, you need to churn out compelling, useful, and unique posts week after week.

But just when a deadline is staring you in the face, it hits: writer's block. It threatens to take away your blogging momentum—and your blog traffic and income along with it.

What can you do when you've run out of things to say?

Kickstart your writing by turning to the blog post ideas in this book, compiled by three blogging aces who've published hundreds of posts between them on websites such as The Huffington Post, Copyblogger, WIRED, and Inc.

The 21 ideas in this book are seeds for blog posts that will grab attention, drive engagement, and make you an unstoppable blogger.

Acknowledgments

From Danny: I know a lot about quitting and becoming an entrepreneur, considering I quit school at age 15 to start my own business. After a few wrong turns, I quit that dead-end startup, but I never gave up on my bigger goal of changing the world through entrepreneurship.

When I started Firepole Marketing (now Mirasee), I wanted to focus on a strong company culture of support, growth, and partnership - a place where people loved their jobs and never wanted to quit. This in turn allows us to fulfill our mission of creating a better world by empowering people through business education.

I want to thank my team for their work and the thousands of entrepreneurs that we've taught to build thriving and sustainable visionary businesses. While every job can't be as awesome as Mirasee, we hope that you find something that is.

From Jim: Growing up, I was firmly taught the "traditional" career path of study hard -> go to college -> get a good job -> eventually retire at 65.

When I was a junior in college, a neighbor friend helped get me an internship at the Bank of Boston. At the end of my second summer he retired after 44 years on the job. He worked there – at the same company – from age 18 to 62!

Clearly that's now a rarity, as job-hopping, corporate restructures, layoffs, and high-flying startups have become the norm.

But it wasn't until 2008 that it seemed possible. While working at WIRED.com, we ran a contest for the greatest self-promoter. The winner was an author I had never heard of, Tim Ferriss, who had launched his *4-Hour Workweek* book less than a year earlier, beating out Steve Jobs, Stephen Colbert, Richard Branson, and Jesus.

He showed me, and millions of others, how to reframe your life and career outside the 9 to 5. More than that, I learned the value of surrounding yourself with people that support your worldview.

So thank you to my family, my friends, my network, and the team members at Mirasee (specifically Rocky Kev and David Kirshbaum) for their continued support in pursuing things you love to do.

Printed in Dunstable, United Kingdom